CASE STUDIES IN

CULTURAL ANTHROPOLOGY

GENERAL EDITORS

George and Louise Spindler

STANFORD UNIVERSITY

THE AINU OF THE NORTHWEST COAST OF SOUTHERN SAKHALIN

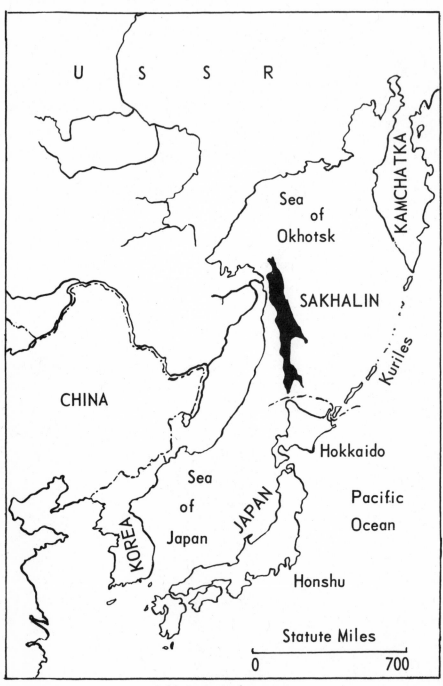

Sakhalin in northeast Asia.

THE AINU OF THE
NORTHWEST COAST
OF SOUTHERN SAKHALIN

By

EMIKO OHNUKI-TIERNEY

University of Wisconsin

HOLT, RINEHART AND WINSTON, INC.

NEW YORK   CHICAGO   SAN FRANCISCO   ATLANTA
DALLAS   MONTREAL   TORONTO   LONDON   SYDNEY

Cover photo: *A bear ceremony, east coast. Photo taken by Pilsudski around 1900 and repro-duced in Paproth (1970). (Courtesy of Paproth)*

Library of Congress Cataloging in Publication Data

Ohnuki-Tierney, Emiko.
The Ainu of the northwest coast of southern Sakhalin.

(Case studies in cultural anthropology)
1. Sakhalin—Ethnology.   2. Ainu.
I. Title.   II. Series.
DK771.S2045   301.29′57′7   74–6281
Bibliography: p. 140
ISBN: 0–03–006926–2

This book is dedicated to

HUSKO and HER AINU PEOPLE

and my parents

KOZABURO and TAKA OHNUKI

Foreword

ABOUT THE SERIES

These case studies in cultural anthropology are designed to bring to students, in beginning and intermediate courses in the social sciences, insights into the richness and complexity of human life as it is lived in different ways and in different places. They are written by men and women who have lived in the societies they write about and who are professionally trained as observers and interpreters of human behavior. The authors are also teachers, and in writing their books they have kept the students who will read them foremost in their minds. It is our belief that when an understanding of ways of life very different from one's own is gained, abstractions and generalizations about social structure, cultural values, subsistence techniques, and the other universal categories of human social behavior become meaningful.

ABOUT THE AUTHOR

Emiko Ohnuki-Tierney received both her M.S. and Ph.D. in anthropology from the University of Wisconsin. After receiving a B.A. in Japan, she came to the United States as a Fulbright exchange student. She has done fieldwork with the Detroit Chinese and the Sakhalin Ainu now resettled in Hokkaido, Japan. Her major interest lies in the subjects related to the perception by a people of their own universe, and her publications include several articles and a book in this area of anthropology. She has taught at the University of Wisconsin, Beloit College, and Marquette University and is presently an Honorary Fellow in the Department of Anthropology, the University of Wisconsin.

ABOUT THE BOOK

Almost everyone has heard of the Ainu and some of the myths, conjectures, and theories about their origins; yet few of us have learned about the Ainu as they are described in this case study. The people pictured in this volume inhabited the northwest coast of southern Sakhalin Island from remote times until the mid-twentieth century. Unfortunately no ethnographic study had been carried out on these Sakhalin Ainu previous to their flight to Hokkaido at the end of World War II. The culture as it is presented in this case study exists in the memory of only a a handful of elders.

Sakhalin is a long narrow island north of Japan, separated from Eurasia by the narrow Strait of Tartar. This land, 589 miles long, with its cold humid climate, is rich in animal and fish life. The Ainu were hunters and gatherers, and in recent times those living in southern Sakhalin probably never amounted to more than about 400 people. This case study demonstrates how a complex cultural tradition can be nurtured and transmitted for generations by a mere handful of people.

Emiko Ohnuki-Tierney has succeeded in providing a detailed account of the Ainu techniques of hunting and gathering, and the use of the materials thus gained, as well as the attitudes and concepts of the Ainu about their environment and their exploitation of it. A reading of this case study should help dispel the notion that hunting and gathering cultures are "simple." To the contrary, the Ainu knowledge of the flora and fauna and ways of making use of them, combined with the rationalization of that use in what we would call religion, together make a very complex and beautifully articulated system. Not only experts in the management of their environment, the Ainu seem to have worked out a harmonious cultural pattern, including the assignment of special meanings to various areas of the interior of the house and to those of the settlement, the assignment of different tasks to men and to women and to the divisions of time. Life has an intricate and self-conscious order: human society is only a part of the universe in which deities, demons, and other beings live in intimate contact with humans. Much of Ainu behavior is devoted to pleasing deities and warding off demons with rituals and taboos. The Ainu are respectful to all soul bearers. Most beings and many things have souls— every Ainu person, every plant, every animal, and most man-made effects have souls—and it is the behavior of the soul, not its appearance, that is important to the Ainu. Respect is therefore a significant aspect of Ainu life.

The Ainu way is full of interest for the reader. The famous bear ceremony, for example, can be easily misunderstood as mere cruelty to a dumb animal since the bear dies slowly in the ritual killing. To the Western reader this death may seem particularly cruel since the bear is usually raised from a cub to one or two years of age for the ritual. The behavior becomes more understandable, however, when it is seen as a ritual of great religious significance, whose purpose is honoring the bear, the supreme deity in the Ainu pantheon. The bear is treated with great kindness and affection before he is dispatched in his second or third year; the ritual, which is described in this case study, is a mark of the great respect in which the bear deity is held.

The author has managed to give a memory culture vitality. It is difficult not to think of the Ainu way as alive and flourishing while reading this book. Her descriptions of events and behaviors have an immediacy that could come only through her intimate relationship with her chief informant, Husko, an aged woman who saw the old way of life intact and was a keen observer of it. This case study also leaves a special impression on us because Emiko Ohnuki-Tierney lets us glimpse now and then her own perceptions and reactions to what she heard and saw.

George and Louise Spindler
General Editors

Portola Valley, Ca.

Acknowledgments

First, I want to thank Husko, my friend and informant, for her warm friendship as well as her patience and genuine interest in the purpose of my work, the recording of the Ainu way. She was proud of the Ainu way, and without her eagerness to teach me, this work would never have materialized. I also express my sincere thanks to all of my Ainu friends in both of my field communities, Wakasakunai and Tokoro, Hokkaido, Japan. Their friendship has been a constant source of encouragement for me, not only during my fieldwork but in subsequent years.

My fieldwork was supported by the National Science Foundation, and I am grateful for their help.

Particular thanks are due to Drs. George and Louise Spindler, who reviewed each chapter thoroughly and promptly. Their efforts were especially important because of my inexperience in English. Above all, I am grateful for their constant and generous encouragement, which made the writing of this case study far easier.

I am most grateful to Professor Toshi Yamamoto, former director of the Sakhalin Museum. The superb quality of his ethnographic work among the east coast Sakhalin Ainu has been a source of inspiration. In 1972, he hand-carried from Japan to Madison, Wisconsin, all of the illustrations, which he originally prepared for his publication, and various Sakhalin Ainu artifacts. He entrusted them to me and gave me his permission to use them in my work.

Special acknowledgment is due to Professor Jan Vansina, whose professional guidance and personal encouragement have been a source of strength during my anthropological career. I am particularly grateful for his review of Chapter 5.

My indebtedness to Professor Chester Chard is long-standing, as well as multifaceted. Not only did he acquire a NSF grant for my fieldwork, but he has continuously supplied me with valuable documents on the Ainu. I am also grateful for his review of Chapter 1. I thank Professor Catharine McClellan for her help and particularly her suggestion that I approach the Ainu culture from the standpoint of world view.

Many thanks are due to Professor Daniel Shea of Beloit College, who so generously took full responsibility for the illustrations. Dr. Tatsuo Kobayashi was most helpful both in providing me with almost inaccessible material on the Ainu and in keeping me informed about recent Japanese publications on the Ainu. His critical review of Chapter 1 was most helpful. I am deeply indebted to Professor Hans-Joachim Paproth for providing detailed bibliographical information on European sources, English translations of some of them, and the use of his photographs. Professor John J. Stephan supplied valuable information on the Ainu and generously reviewed Chapter 1. I am indebted to many other scholars who contributed to my Ainu study, including Professors Shinichiro Takakura, Shiro Hattori, Toshio

ix

Oba, Hitoshi Watanabe, Kioe Yonemura, Hideo Fujimoto, Sakuzaemon Kodama, George Kodama, Mari Kodama, Hiroaki Okada, and Atsuko Okada.

I am thankful to the following friends who proofread portions of my manuscript: Ms. Elizabeth Reinartz, Ms. Alison Drucker, Dr. Glenda Denniston, and Dr. Jon P. Tierney. I am most grateful to Ms. Thelma Bennett, who typed the entire manuscript despite her ill health and the recent loss of her husband.

Many thanks are due also to Mr. David Boynton and to Ms. Kathleen Nevils of Holt, Rinehart and Winston for their most efficient and kind assistance in the production of this book. Finally, I would like to thank my husband Tim, who rendered help in many ways and, above all, made our home atmosphere suitable for writing.

E. O-T.

Ainu Phonemes

Ainu spoken on the northwest coast and used in this book includes the following phonemes:

vowels: /i, e, a, o, u/

length: /:/

consonants: /p, t, k, č, s, m, n, r, h, w, y/

Vowels:

	Front	Central	Back
High	i		u
Mid	e		o
Low		a	

English approximation

/i/ as in s*i*t

/e/ as in b*e*t

/a/ as in r*o*d

/o/ as in *o*bey

/u/ as in p*u*t

Consonants: Most consonants have approximately the same values as in English. However, a brief discussion of some of them is in order. /p, t, k/ are "perhaps" in free variation with voiced allophones [p, d, g]. Usually these stops are voiceless at the initial position. In some words, however, they are pronounced as voiceless and in some as voiced regardless of the position. There also are words that are pronounced with either a voiceless stop or a voiced stop. On the whole, words with a voiceless stop at any position outnumber those with a voiced stop. /č/, as in the English word *church*, is in free variation with a voiced allophone [ǰ], as in *j*uice. /s/ becomes highly palatalized before or after /i/. /r/ is a short voiced alveolar flap. /h/ is a voiceless glottal fricative and is pronounced very softly when it is at the final position. (For a detailed discussion of Ainu phonemes, see Ohnuki-Tierney 1969b:5–8.)

Contents

Sakhalin Ainu in front of an Ainu house (circa 1900). (Courtesy of C. Chard)

Sakhalin Ainu in 1912. The women are wearing the fish skin garments. The man second from the left wears a fur cap of the neighboring Orok people. (Courtesy of George and Mari Kodama)

1 / Introduction

"The hairy Ainu," "the Caucasoid race in the Far East," "the lost tribes of Israel," "the Far Eastern relatives of the Australian aborigines," "stone age savages" —these are only a few of the many labels outsiders applied to the Ainu when their presence off the northeastern corner of the vast Eurasian continent became widely known during the nineteenth century. These striking people with deep-set eyes and abundant body hair fascinated both scholars and laymen. They resembled Caucasoid peoples and looked distinctly different from the Chinese, Koreans, and Japanese with classical Mongoloid features who are the major occupants of that corner of the Far East. To others their appearance suggested a relation to the Australian aborigines, although none of the Negroid features of the latter were present among the Ainu. Not only their appearance but also their language was enigmatic—unintelligible to outsiders and seemingly unrelated to any other known language. In addition, they were a hunting and gathering people living in small scattered settlements, in sharp contrast to the neighboring agricultural populations. Thus, along with the Tasmanians, Australians, and a few others, the Ainu soon became one of the "classics" in anthropological literature. With the encroaching "civilized" peoples already threatening to engulf the Ainu culture and biological identity, ethnologists, physical anthropologists, archaeologists, historians, and linguists all began studies of their contemporary lift and enigmatic past.

The sustained interest which the Ainu hold as a people is partially due to their puzzling identity, the problem to be addressed in the next section of this chapter. Yet, beyond this, the Ainu way of life has a certain beauty which easily can become a source of fascination to students of Ainu culture, like myself. A senior scholar in the field once remarked to me that everyone initiating an Ainu study regrets that he did not start earlier, and yet finds years later that the field is still attracting novices, despite the fact that the Ainu way of life now exists primarily in the memories of older people.

Fearless hunters on land and sea, the Ainu nevertheless maintained a tradition of aesthetic sensitivity. They produced beautiful and highly stylized epic poems, whose superb literary quality is considered comparable to those of the Greeks. Their oral tradition was indeed rich and well developed. Many volumes of their epic poems, while fortunately recorded before the deaths of capable narrators, are little known outside Japan, because the translations are primarily in Japanese. The sensitivity of the Ainu to beauty in life was also expressed in skillful woodcarvings by men

1

and appliqué, embroidery, and weaving by women, who in addition were almost comparable to trained botanists in their knowledge of local vegetation. Although many circumpolar peoples deify bears, the Ainu were one of only a few peoples whose elaborate bear ceremonialism included raising of cubs for rituals (Hallo-well 1926).

The Ainu homeland in the recent past consisted of the islands of Hokkaido, southern Sakhalin, and the Kuriles, although their territory once included southern Kamchatka, the northern part of the main Japanese island (Honshu), and possibly northern Sakhalin and the lower Amur region (frontispiece). All of these groups comprised a population that basically shared an Ainu way of life and language. The Hokkaido Ainu are the largest group of all, and perhaps the best known in the English-speaking world. The Sakhalin Ainu who inhabited southern Sakhalin are now relocated in Hokkaido, since the land became U.S.S.R. territory at the end of World War II. The Kurile Ainu are now extinct.

This book is about the way of life of those Ainu who during the first half of the twentieth century inhabited the northwest coast of southern Sakhalin, between *Rayčiska*[1] and the former Russo-Japanese border (Fig. 1). Together with the rest of the Sakhalin Ainu, they are now relocated in Hokkaido. Consequently, the way of life described in this book now exists only in the cognitive maps and the memory of a handful of elders.

WHO ARE THE AINU?—AN ENIGMA

Although this book is an ethnographic description of the northwest coast Sakhalin Ainu, the racial and cultural identity of the Ainu is first briefly discussed, since the problem of Ainu identity is not only intriguing in itself but holds one of the keys to a broader anthropological problem—the peopling of both the Old and New Worlds. Geographically, the Ainu occupy a most strategic location through which early migrants may have passed from the Old World to the New. Are the Ainu, then, one of the peoples who stayed behind as other big-game hunters crossed the Bering Straits to the New World? Or do they represent a population which claimed the land even earlier, as Birdsell (1951) maintains? Are they so-called genetic remnants like the Negritos, as Chard (1968) proposes? Or are they related to any of the prehistoric populations in the area? The difficulty of answering this last question is compounded by the fact that we still do not know the relationship of the present-day Japanese to the prehistoric populations of the Japanese archipelago. A multitude of questions thus arises in connection with Ainu identity.

Earlier propositions concerning Ainu racial affiliation were based on the physical characteristics of the living Ainu and on skeletal material which was identified as that of the recent Ainu on the basis of burial goods and other evidence. Investigations then aimed at placing the Ainu into one of the few and broad racial classifications—an approach which is now considered of dubious value. For

---

[1] All italicized Ainu terms are in phonemic notation.

example, wavy hair, abundant body hair, a frequent lack of the epicanthic fold, and a well-developed chin were features frequently cited by scholars who advocated the Caucasoid affiliation of the Ainu. The wavy hair tended to be most conspicuous in males who grew long beards, while lack of the epicanthic fold of the upper eyelid, which gives the eyes of Mongoloid peoples their distinctive slitlike appearance, singled out the Ainu from the surrounding peoples. Other scholars emphasized

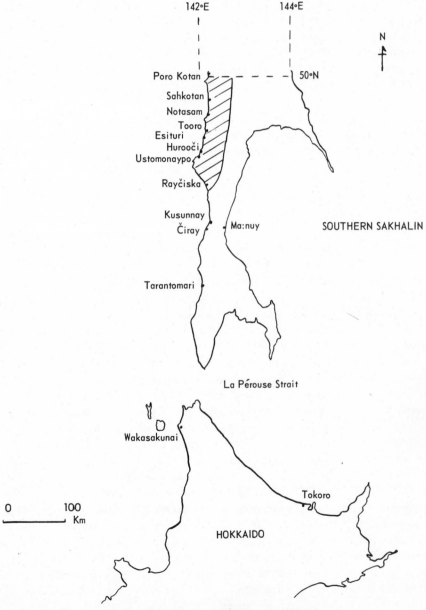

Figure 1. Southern Sakhalin and Hokkaido.

Mongoloid characteristics in the Ainu and proposed their Mongoloid affiliation, while most of the Soviet scholars enhanced the Australo-Oceanic classification (Levin 1963). Thus, scholars' opinions were widely divided.

More recently, serological analyses have been made to clarify Ainu racial affiliation. Some of these studies (Omoto 1974; Spuhler 1966) concluded that the Ainu show a closer affinity to Mongoloid populations in the area than they do to the peoples of either Europe or Australia. However, the results of serological studies cannot be conclusive, since most of the contemporary Ainu are actually of mixed ancestry of various sorts.

Another significant approach to the problem has been to trace the Ainu, as a people and as a culture, step by step through archaeological stages on the Japanese archipelago. In Table 1, the archaeological sequences of the right-hand column have been established primarily on the basis of Hokkaido archaeology. Because of the present political status of Sakhalin, we know little of its archaeology. However, many scholars seem to believe that southern Sakhalin was basically in the cultural sphere of Hokkaido, although the region was no doubt exposed also to influences from the Asian continent (Yoshizaki 1963:145).

We are fairly certain that a continuity in culture, physical type, and language may be traced from the beginning of the agricultural (Yayoi) period to the present day. Thus, the Yayoi agricultural population in southwestern Japan was very likely ancestral to the modern Japanese. However, we still are not sure of the identity of the occupants of the archipelago during the preagricultural periods. The problem of the linkage between pre- and postagricultural cultures on the Japanese archipelago is directly related to the question of the Ainu identity: Are one or both populations, the Ainu and the historic Japanese, derived from the preagricultural populations?

One recently proposed hypothesis which has been well received by scholars is that the Ainu are the descendants of a segment of the preagricultural (Jomon) population in northern Japan. The picture of the past of the Japanese archipelago which emerges from this hypothesis is that the major portions of the islands were first—possibly around 30,000 B.C.—occupied by a hunting-gathering people or peoples in small scattered settlements. Around 10,000 B.C. these inhabitants became the earliest known pottery makers in the world, although they remained ignorant of agriculture for a long time. By 300 B.C., but possibly as early as 600 B.C., rice agriculture was introduced on the archipelago's main island (Honshu), perhaps by way of the Korean Peninsula, and possibly from southeast Asia. It is generally accepted that the introduction of agricultural techniques at this time was accompanied by little or no immigration of other peoples. At its inception, rice agriculture penetrated neither into the northeastern half of the main island nor into Hokkaido and Sakhalin. The rejection of agriculture in these regions is ascribed partially to the cold climate but more to a cultural basis. That is, there were basic differences between the cultures of the southwest and those of the northeast, and the latter were not receptive to agriculture. Subsequently agriculture spread farther north but never reached Hokkaido or Sakhalin.

In any event, the cultures on the main island where agriculture had penetrated started to change rapidly. While these agricultural populations on the main island

TABLE 1   THE AINU AND ARCHAEOLOGICAL STAGES
ON THE JAPANESE ARCHIPELAGO

	Main Island	Hokkaido and Sakhalin	
		Historic Ainu	A.D. 1300
	Historic period	Satsumon culture (hunting and gathering; pit dwelling; hearth; cooking fire; ironware)	
		(Okhotsk culture) *	A.D. 700– 800
A.D. 550	Japanese nation	Post-Jomon culture (hunting and gathering; metal use)	
A.D. 300	Tomb period (state formation)		
	Agricultural (Yayoi) culture		100 B.C.
300 B.C.		Jomon ceramic culture (hunting and gathering)	
	Jomon ceramic culture (hunting and gathering)		
10,000 B.C.			5000 B.C.
	Preceramic culture (hunting and gathering)	Preceramic culture (hunting and gathering)	
30,000 B.C.			

* The Okhotsk culture, which appeared and disappeared rather suddenly and enigmatically, is considered by many scholars as an intrusive culture.

were in the process of forming denser settlements, then states, and finally the Japanese nation, the groups to the north continued their way of life by hunting and gathering natural resources from land and water. Their culture(s), too, however, changed over time. The introduction of the use of metal in these nonagricultural areas through trade thus marked a new archaeological stage, the Post-Jomon. Some elements in this culture at least suggest Ainu affinity. For example, the Post-Jomon people used a bear motif in decorations on pottery and bone implements. Skeletal material at some Post-Jomon sites is reported to show a close affinity to the Ainu in northeastern Hokkaido (Yamaguchi 1963a:131–146; 1963b:55–71). Around A.D. 700–800, this Post-Jomon culture developed into what is called the Satsumon culture, characterized by semisubterranean pits, hearths, and cooking fires like those used by the Ainu. The Ainu and the Satsumon people also share such cultural traits as mode of burial and a special type of pottery character-ized by handles attached to the interior surface of a pot. There is thus an indication that all these peoples (Post-Jomon, Satsumon, and Ainu) may represent one population whose subsistence economy consisted of hunting and fishing along the coasts and in rivers and lakes (for further details, see Fujimoto 1971; Sakurai 1967).

Since the Post-Jomon culture must have derived from the Jomon culture, it is logical to conclude that, according to this hypothesis, the Ainu should have derived ultimately from at least a segment of the former Jomon population. However, proof of the continuity of Ainu culture from Jomon culture is still highly tenuous. Relatively certain continuity in terms of culture and people has been established only between the Ainu on the one hand and the Satsumon and Post-Jomon peoples on the other.

The above hypothesis about the Ainu identity presents one difficulty, however. Carried to its logical conclusion, it can point to a common sharing of ancestors by the Ainu and Japanese; that is, both populations are held to derive from the Jomon people. But if this is the case, how do we account for the differences in physical types between the two populations as we see them today? It seems problematic to ascribe the differences solely to the separate development of the two peoples since the beginning of the Yayoi agricultural period. An alternative explanation suggested by some scholars is that the ancestors of the Japanese and the Ainu were two different populations who shared a common culture. That is, the ancestors of the Ainu were a non-Jomon population of northern Japan, or more specifically northeastern Hokkaido, who received considerable cultural in-fluences from the Jomon culture. Paucity of prehistoric Ainu skeletal material has had a crippling effect on the investigation of the Ainu as a population through time. There are some sketetal features such as long- to medium-headedness and the rectangular shape of the eye sockets which tend to characterize the recent Ainu, in contrast to the short-headed Japanese with round eye sockets. However, there is much variation in physical types among the historic Ainu, let alone among any of the populations represented in archaeological stages.

There have been continuing controversies among scholars about the problem of Ainu identity and its relation to Japanese archaeology, so that what is described above is merely a bare outline of one of the most well-accepted propositions on Ainu prehistory (see, for example, Howells 1966 for an alternative interpretation). In any event, the original Ainu homeland seems to have been Hokkaido, most likely the northeastern half of it, with the Ainu later expanding their territory to include adjacent areas. When and by which route they originally arrived in the Japanese archipelago are other controversial questions among scholars. Generally speaking, proponents of the Caucasoid affiliation of the Ainu seem fewer in number at present. Some suggest the Ainu affiliation with the Archaic Caucasoid (Birdsell 1951), while a great number of scholars (Hanihara 1974; Howells 1966; Omoto

1974; Spuhler 1966) seem to link the Ainu with the Mongoloid populations in the area.

The Ainu language is as enigmatic as the people and the rest of their culture. The confusion about its genetic affiliation is compounded by the fact that in the area surrounding the Ainu homeland there are four isolated languages—Ainu, Korean, Japanese, and Gilyak—all of whose genetic affiliations to other languages are in doubt or unknown. Some "speculate" that Ainu, Japanese, and Korean may be descendants of a sister language to Proto-Altaic, a linguistic stock which is ancestral to such languages as Mongolian, Manchu, Tungus, and Turkic (see, for example, Street 1962).

After a century of this quest for Ainu identity we are still far from our goal. In the process of inquiry, however, we have gained better understanding of the Ainu people and their culture and also have come to grips with such fundamental anthropological problems as which aspects of culture may be considered least susceptible to change and hence may be used as indexes for the identification of a particular group of people.

SAKHALIN AINU: THEIR PAST ON SAKHALIN

We do not know for certain when the Sakhalin Ainu first arrived in southern Sakhalin. We do know, however, that for the past several hundred years the Ainu have occupied the southern half of the island, approximately south of 50 degrees north latitude, with the remainder in the hands of the Gilyak. There is also a small number of other "native" peoples on the island, such as Oroks and Nanays, as they are now called in the U.S.S.R. Our best guess is that the Ainu moved to the island from Hokkaido (Chard 1968), possibly as early as the first millennium A.D., but definitely by the thirteenth century.

Censuses of the Sakhalin Ainu, taken at different points in time between the end of the nineteenth century and 1945, have given populations of from 1200 to 2400 (the Hokkaido Ainu by comparison are estimated at between 15,000 and 17,000). These census figures include all who have any Ainu "blood" or ancestry, no matter how little. Often, however, the counts neglect to include those Ainu in remote areas, such as the settlements on the northwest coast, and thus are not reliable.

Sakhalin's wealth of natural resources had the unfortunate consequence of luring traders and, later, colonial powers. Although Sakhalin is located on the northeastern extremity of Far Eastern civilization and is even separated by water from the Eurasian continent, travelers from interior China can use the natural communication routes of the Sungari, Ussuri, and Amur rivers to reach the mouth of the Amur, from where they can cross the narrow Tartar Strait to Sakhalin either by boat or, during winter when the strait is frozen, by dog sled.

Chinese influence reached the island by this natural route, perhaps indirectly through other natives along the Amur acting as middlemen, possibly as early as the first millennium A.D. Chinese influence, however, intensified during the thirteenth century when northern Sakhalin submitted to Mongol suzerainty subsequent to the Mongol conquest of China. The period between 1263 and 1320 saw Mongol colonization and the "pacification" of the Gilyak and Ainu. Although the Gilyak readily submitted to Mongol forces, the Sakhalin Ainu fought valiantly until 1308 when the last of the Sakhalin Ainu chiefs submitted to the sovereignty of the Yüan dynasty, the Mongols who were ruling China. Then the Ainu too started to pay tribute to the Mongols. From the fifteenth century, the trade along the Amur and on Sakhalin gradually merged with the Japanese-Hokkaido Ainu trade which had been going on for some time.

This trade reached its height during the eighteenth century. During this period, the Manchus, who had conquered the Chinese, involved all the natives along the Amur and on Sakhalin in sending tribute missions to Manchu posts on the Amur River. The Sakhalin Ainu presented the Manchus with fur, especially marten, and eagle feathers, dried fish, and other products of their own as well as Japanese iron-ware. In return they received from the Manchus brocade, beads, cotton material, pipes, and needles, some of which they traded to the Japanese. The Ainu received from the Japanese rice, rice wine, tobacco, and ironware. The trade was carried out in stages involving all the "natives" in the area, many of whom served as middlemen. As a result, Japanese ironware reached the Manchu and, conversely, treasured Chinese brocade and cotton made their way to Osaka in western Japan. Not only the Manchus and Japanese took advantage of the Ainu in this trade; even the other peoples who acted as middlemen exploited them. The Gilyak were said to have been especially cruel to the Ainu, enslaving those who failed to pay their debts (for details of the trade, see Harrison 1954; Takakura 1939).

Toward the end of the eighteenth century, Manchu control over Sakhalin dwindled rapidly, and at the very beginning of the nineteenth century the tribute system was discontinued. By then, however, both the Japanese and the Russian governments were approaching Sakhalin with an accelerated speed, each racing to take political control of the island and monopolize its natural resources. There followed a century and a half of territorial conflict between the two countries, and the fate of the Sakhalin Ainu fell into the hands of these two nations.

To its credit, however, in 1809, the Japanese government paid all the debts which the Ainu owed to others who served as middlemen in the trade system and assumed all responsibility for the Ainu. Needless to say, the Japanese government was motivated by self-interest. It resorted to this action believing that the exploitation of the Ainu by others would lead to Manchu control of the Ainu, since these middlemen were supposedly official Manchu government representatives whose duty it was to collect tributes. At any rate, the action by the Japanese government alleviated the Ainu situation considerably.

The impact of the Japanese government on the Ainu intensified with the establishment of the Meiji regime in Japan in 1868, after which Japanese exploitation of natural resources in Sakhalin proceeded rapidly. To facilitate this process, the government brought many Japanese immigrants to the island. Ainu labor was also needed, so that Japanese officials assumed direct administrative and judicial control over the Ainu. Under the new governmental policy of assimilating the Ainu, the latter were not only granted equal status with Japanese but those Ainu on the southern and eastern coasts even received the same education as Japanese. The government also encouraged the Ainu to use the Japanese language, which they had been forbidden to speak prior to 1871.

The Japanization of southern Sakhalin, however, was interrupted during the period 1875–1905, when southern Sakhalin came under Russian control. The fate of the Ainu was once again at the mercy of outside powers, who decided that Japan should control all of the Kurile Island chain while Russia should claim the entire island of Sakhalin.

In 1875, as the Russians moved southward, burning houses and looting, 843 Sakhalin Ainu on the southern and eastern coasts made the difficult decision to leave their homeland for Japanese territory and asked the Japanese government to sponsor their relocation. These Ainu, called Tsuishikari Ainu because of their new location at Tsuishikari near Sapporo in Hokkaido, found their adjustment in the new environment harder than they had anticipated. In 1886–1887 smallpox epidemics and in 1886 a cholera epidemic took a high death toll. Some of the migrants returned to Sakhalin, albeit unwillingly, even before 1905. The remaining 395 Ainu also returned to their original homeland at the conclusion of the Russo-Japanese War, when southern Sakhalin was reclaimed by Japan as the result of her victory over Russia.

The period of Russian occupation of southern Sakhalin was one of complete chaos for all concerned, especially during the period 1881–1905, when the entire island was utilized as one large penal colony by tsarist Russia.

The period between the termination of the Russo-Japanese War and the end of World War II was one of intensive Japanization of the Ainu, especially those in the southern and eastern portions of southern Sakhalin. During the years between 1912 and 1914, the Japanese government gathered the Ainu from their traditional settlements and placed them in a limited number of locations so that it could better "protect" them. Needless to say, the effect of this relocation on the Ainu way of life was profound. However, the northwest coast, which had been left relatively untouched by the Japanese governmental operations because of its remoteness, was again exempt from this process. As time went on, more and more major Japanese industries employing many Ainu males were established. Toward the end of World War II, southern Sakhalin became the northern frontier, and the Japanese government could not exploit the natural resources of the area fast enough for war purposes. Simultaneously, many Ainu males were enlisted either voluntarily or involuntarily in the Japanese military forces.

This Japanization process came to a violent end in 1945. As the Russians moved into southern Sakhalin to reoccupy the area, many Ainu and Japanese fled in their fishing boats across the Soya (La Pérouse) Strait to Hokkaido. Some chose to remain in Sakhalin, but the rest of the Ainu, together with the Japanese migrants, were relocated in Hokkaido by the Japanese government shortly after the war.

The above discussion is only the briefest sketch of the rich but turbulent past of the Sakhalin Ainu (for details of the history of Sakhalin, see Stephan 1971). Without adding any more details about historical events, I shall now briefly assess the effects of these events on the Ainu. Since there is much regional variation in Ainu culture, and historical events affected the Ainu in each region differently, I shall confine my discussion to the Ainu of the northwest coast of southern Sakhalin, about whom this book is written.

In terms of outside influence on Ainu culture, the trade system may have had a fairly significant effect on the Ainu of the northwest coast. It seems, however, to have affected primarily the Ainu material culture, and trade goods were used mainly as status symbols or offerings to the deities. Of all the peoples who featured in the history of the island, the Gilyak seem to have exerted the most influence on the Ainu of the northwest coast. The Ainu and Gilyak shared a basic subsistence economy of hunting and gathering. They had been geographical neighbors for a long time, and in a few settlements near the former Russo-Japanese border the two peoples even resided in the same settlements, each occupying a section. Despite the record of Gilyak exploitation of the Ainu through trade, the northwest coast Ainu view the Gilyak in a more favorable light than the other peoples with whom they have interacted. There were a few cases of intermarriage, and the Ainu consider the Gilyak to be distantly related to them, while they regard other peoples as entirely different. Some cultural exchange between the two peoples had apparently taken place. However, their two ways of life were clearly distinct and each people kept its own identity.

In contrast to the rest of the Ainu on Sakhalin, those of the northwest coast had a friendly attitude toward the Russians. These Ainu were not involved in the emigration to Hokkaido in 1895. Some of them were employed by Russians in herding and fishing enterprises. The two ways of life, however, were quite different, and cultural exchange between the two peoples was limited. One aspect of Russian technology, however, made a significant impact on Ainu life—the technique of building warm Russian-style cabins. This technique not only replaced the traditional Ainu method of building houses but resulted in discontinuance of the pattern of seasonal movement by the Ainu. Until around the turn of the twentieth century, the Ainu spent the summer in coastal settlements and then moved to an interior location where they spent the winter in semisubterranean houses. With the introduction of Russian techniques they were able to build their summer houses warm enough to permit winter occupancy. This change in the pattern of life, however, does not seem to have made a significant impact on other aspects of their life, which continued to be based on the dual system of summer fishing and winter hunting.

The northwest coast was the area Japanese influence reached least and latest. Although Japanese government officials had been in the area since 1858, and the first of the Japanese industries had penetrated by 1924, the Ainu and the Japanese lived in generally peaceful coexistence in their separate settlements. Contact was confined to Ainu males who worked in Japanese industries. Attendance at Japanese schools, strongly imposed on the rest of the Sakhalin Ainu, was not mandatory here. Most significant, the northwest coast Ainu were not involved in the two major shifts of the Ainu population of Sakhalin—the Ainu emigration to Tsuishikari in Hokkaido in 1875 and the 1912–1914 resettlement of the Ainu into certain locations. Therefore, the situation of the northwest coast Ainu contrasts significantly with that of the rest of the Sakhalin Ainu, on whom the Japanese had a profound impact during the twentieth century.

Perhaps one of the most important basic reasons the northwest coast Ainu were able to retain their way of life was the small size of both the total population and the individual settlements. Both Russians and Japanese were interested primarily in political control of the Ainu and economic exploitation in the form of Ainu labor. Due to the sparse population, the Ainu political structure on the northwest coast was informal and most activities were carried out by individual families or kin groups. Therefore, the changes forced upon the Ainu political structure by the Japanese government had less effect on Ainu life here than elsewhere. Too, because the region was the least populated and the farthest from Hokkaido, exploitation of the northwest coast and its labor force was relatively unattractive to the Japanese government.

Perhaps it is the material culture of the Ainu which underwent the most significant changes as a result of these contacts with other peoples. Yet most of the foreign objects obtained by the Ainu, such as Chinese brocade and Japanese lacquerware, were used primarily as status symbols and as offerings to deities rather than as effects of everyday existence. In short, the Ainu way of life remained basically intact due to the Ainu reinterpretation of foreign influences in terms of their own cultural patterns.

The above statement by no means implies that the Ainu culture on the northwest coast has been static; by contrast, as with every culture, it has experienced constant change in conjunction with both internal and external stimuli. The Ainu culture of the northwest coast, however, seems to have had enough plasticity and strength to withstand the impact of neighboring peoples without being shattered.

SAKHALIN: LOCATION AND NATURAL HABITAT

Sakhalin is a long, narrow island located north of Japan and along the coast of the Eurasian continent from which it is separated only by the narrow Tartar Strait (see frontispiece). It is 589 miles in length and 28,597 square miles in area, roughly comparable to Ireland in size. It lies between 141 degrees 38 minutes and 144 degrees 55 minutes east longitude and between 45 degrees 54 minutes and 54 degrees 24 minutes north latitude. Except for two sizable interior plains, southern Sakhalin is mountainous. Its climate is severely cold and humid during many months of the year, with an average temperature in the south of 17 degrees F in January and 63 degrees F in July.

The island is extremely rich in natural resources. Its coasts, rivers, and lakes abound in salmon, trout, herring, cod, and king crab as well as seals and other sea mammals. Whales are also abundant, although they come primarily to the southern coasts. The land also has a diverse assortment of fauna and flora. The bear is the most impressive, but there are also musk deer, reindeer, otter, marten, fox, and several other fur bearers. Out of a flora of one thousand species, ninety-five are trees such as larch, fir, spruce, and birch. Although not of concern to the Ainu, the island is also rich in coal, iron, gold, silver, and other metals as well as oil and natural gas.

SAKHALIN AINU AFTER WORLD WAR II

The final and devastating conclusion of the political and military struggle between Japan and the U.S.S.R. in 1945 abruptly terminated the Ainu way of life in the land they had occupied since the time of their remote ancestors. As I noted earlier, many Ainu left Sakhalin to resettle in Hokkaido. The Japanese government placed them, together with Japanese settlers returning from Sakhalin, in underdeveloped areas of Hokkaido in order that they might exploit the natural resources. They were provided with free housing, land, and capital to start their new life.

Most of the Sakhalin Ainu chose to settle in coastal areas to make fishing their occupation. However, during subsequent years, catches of herring, salmon, and other fish declined drastically, making life quite difficult for the Ainu. Many of their young men seek employment at more prosperous fishing ports and during the nonfishing season obtain jobs as lumberjacks or as crew members in ocean fishing boats. Women, especially young girls, also seek employment in the cities of Hokkaido since their small fishing communities provide no jobs for them.

A Soviet source (Stephan 1971: 193) reports that 600 Sakhalin Ainu remain on the island and that they are now organized into fishing cooperatives in eight settlements in the southern parts of Sakhalin. This population figure seems rather high, but I have no way of cross-checking it.

FIELDWORK

My fieldwork was done over a period of a year (1965–1966) and, later, three months (1969) spent in two communities in Hokkaido, Wakasakunai, and Tokoro, where Sakhalin Ainu are resettled. When I set out to learn about the Ainu way of life in 1965, I selected Wakasakunai in the northwestern tip of Hokkaido, since with a population of about 160 Sakhalin Ainu, it constituted the largest such community in Japan. The Ainu here were mostly from the southern portion of southern Sakhalin, where the Japanese had penetrated most intensively and in the greatest numbers. Thus these people had been amply exposed to Japanese prejudice. The problem was intensified in Wakasakunai, where the Ainu were put into direct economic and social competition in the same community with the Japanese who had also been expatriated from Sakhalin. As a result, these Ainu chose not to be identified as Ainu. Having been born in western Japan where the Ainu were romantic but distant figures, I had underestimated both the amount of prejudice among local Japanese and the intensity of the negative feeling about their own identity that I would encounter among the Ainu themselves. Thus quite naively I tried my best to explain that I was there to learn their way because I respected it. I also tried to be of some practical help by teaching English to their children—English being compulsory from the seventh grade in Japanese public schools.

Eventually I decided to leave Wakasakunai. My decision came partly from my deep feeling of respect for an Ainu who in his thirties became the leader of the Japanese-Ainu community. Thoroughly aware of his fellow-Ainus' ambivalent feelings toward my presence in the community, he took full responsibility for my being there. He was an extremely intelligent man and, although illiterate, was acutely interested in matters beyond his community. I enjoyed discussing such matters as the Kennedy assassination and its implications with him. He wanted me to study how the Ainu in the community under his leadership had risen to positions equal to or above those of the Japanese. As I became better acquainted with him and other Ainu who personally treated me with the warmest of feelings, I felt compelled to respect their preference for not being identified as Ainu. Furthermore, I was more interested in recording the Ainu way of life before it vanished forever—even from memory—than I was in studying the contemporary adaptation of this community. Since practically all of the Ainu in the community were from the strongly acculturated southern portion of southern Sakhalin, I could not find good informants for this purpose even among older people.

I then visited an Ainu woman in Tokoro at the eastern end of Hokkaido who was considered by linguists as a valuable informant on one of the Sakhalin Ainu dialects. In no time at all I was convinced that she was an extremely valuable source of information on the Ainu way of life, and thereafter I spent most of my time with her. On days when she was not feeling well, I also visited other Sakhalin Ainu in the community. She was proud of the Ainu way of life and was as eager a teacher as I was a student. She often exhausted me and I exhausted her, about which we often laughed.

This woman, whom I shall refer to by her nickname Husko ("ancient"), was born in 1900 in a winter settlement near Esituri and spent most of her life on the northwest coast of southern Sakhalin. Both her paternal and maternal ancestors had lived for many generations in the area. She was very shy when young and preferred to be with her parents and older people rather than with her age group. From these older Ainu she learned the Ainu way of life more thoroughly than did most of her contemporaries. She was especially close to her father who took pride in doing things the Ainu way. Although there were Japanese in the area, they were in separate communities and she had very little, although friendly, contact with them.

She married, during the latter part of her teens, an Ainu who later became chief of the Ainu settlement at *Rayčiska*, one of the largest settlements on the northwest coast. She had five children by him. Three of them died when they were quite young, and two of her daughters and their families now reside near her in Tokoro. From the beginning of World War II she came in frequent contact with Japanese officials through her husband and learned her second language—Japanese. In 1941 her husband died. Four years later she married another Ainu and moved to his settlement of *Tarantomari* on the southwestern coast. She remained there until her emigration to Hokkaido after the war.

Husko has an exceptionally keen mind. She is eager to learn what is going on and why and is quick to grasp a situation. For example, noticing my typewritten pages, she asked me if they were the product of the machine she had watched on television. Although she does not read or write, she wanted me to teach her and her grandchildren a few English words. I am sure her wealth of knowledge of the Ainu life owes much to her inquiring attitude and intelligence. I appreciated her knowledge of her own culture, especially upon recalling how often I had to resort to written sources to find answers to questions on Japan from my American friends. Only those individuals gifted with a relentlessly inquisitive mind are good informants about their own culture.

During much of our time together she related to me what she remembered. Her information was richest when she chose what she was to tell me, although I had many specific questions during my second fieldwork in 1969 to fill "holes" in my 1965–1966 field data. She also made many small models of garments, a cradle, footgear, and headgear in order to show me how they were made. She was exceptionally good at sewing and embroidery and made several garments for me. On fine days when her injured hip was not giving her too much pain we went plant gathering. On a few occasions we also went for a walk on the beach near her home; the first task of the day for Ainu women is to survey the beach to see if there are freshly killed fish, sea mammals, or birds which are of use. She also was a shamaness and I had opportunities to observe her rites.

Traditional ethnographic methods include participant observation, by which an anthropologist does as nearly as possible what a member of the host society would do. For my "salvage ethnography," however, this method had only limited applicability. Furthermore, I found out quite unexpectedly that one unorthodox approach was rather successful; that was to make mistakes. For example, once I was much involved in talking with Husko and several other Ainu visitors at her house when I suddenly felt something warm next to my lap. Without giving a thought I grabbed it; it was a baby mouse. I jumped several feet off the ground, spilling tea from a cup nearby. Husko reprimanded me rather strongly. She said only a foolish person got frightened easily, and when someone was easily frightened, evil spirits would try to enter that person. Again, during my second fieldwork in 1969, I was in the later stages of pregnancy and my husband visited me in the field. During this period, I made all manner of mistakes in terms of proper behavior as a pregnant woman and in terms of a woman's attitude toward her husband. Thus, there was a steady flow of information from Husko, her family members, and friends on what a pregnant woman should and should not do and how a woman should treat her husband, much of which might never have come out had I not made so many mistakes. Best of all, however, was Husko's dried-up bear intestine, a charm to insure a safe delivery. She had saved this for years and yet gave it very generously to me, her rather clumsy "daughter." Also, I sensed that basically they wanted me to be myself; although they came to understand my respect for their way of life, they knew that I belonged to a different society.

Even though my situation did not lend itself to this method, I do not underestimate the validity of participant observation. Indeed, on many occasions the people were delighted at my attempts to do things the Ainu way. However, even when I made a mistake they were eager to correct me, and they also enjoyed comparison, especially the three-way comparison of doing the same thing differently—the Ainu, the Japanese, and the American way.

SCOPE OF THIS BOOK

Although this book covers most of the aspects of the Ainu life as any ethnographic case study would, I have tried to present the Ainu way as the Ainu themselves see it. I have put it in the frame of their perception of their universe—how they picture it, how they dissect and classify its parts, and how they think and feel about these parts as well as about the universe as a whole. One of the strongest reasons for this type of presentation is not because of my theoretical training in anthropology but because of my own experience in the field. The revelation for this approach came on the first day of plant gathering. As we stepped out of Husko's house on a fine early spring morning to gather plants in the field next to her house, I realized that the promontories in her mental picture of the grass field and those in mine were entirely different. Despite her age, she spotted every edible and medicinal plant well beyond the scope of my eyesight. Furthermore, she went directly to plants whose useful parts were well developed. The Ainu find different uses for different parts of a plant and thus they have different labels for each part, as we shall see later. Needless to say, my experience in both Japanese and American culture enabled me only to spot colorful flowers, which are of no concern to the Ainu. Thus my aesthetic elevation on a fine spring morning was tinged with sadness and feelings of inadequacy as a student of a new culture. As time went on I became more and more convinced that I should learn the Ainu concept of the Ainu way.

In the following pages, I try to translate, as it were, how and why the Ainu consider hunting a religious experience; how they have an equivalent of capital punishment for human beings as a code and yet exercise it in practice only on "delinquent" deities (bears) who kill humans; and the like. Given the size of this book, my account of Ainu life has to leave out many details. However, I shall try to describe their way of life with particular attention to individual variations and norms versus actual behavior patterns.

As I noted earlier, this book concerns only the Ainu who inhabited the northwest coast of southern Sakhalin during the first half of the twentieth century. The way of life presented in this book essentially exists in the memory of a handful of elders. Unfortunately, no ethnographic study was carried out among this group of Sakhalin Ainu while they were on their own land.

This study does not attempt to cover all of the Sakhalin Ainu, let alone the Ainu in general. There is a high degree of intracultural variation among the Ainu whose land was often separated by sea and mountains from fellow-Ainu in another region. A discussion of regional differences is beyond the scope of this study. At the end of the book is a selected list of references for readers interested in Ainu in other regions.

Photographs of Sakhalin Ainu in any region are very rare. However, thanks to some colleagues, I was fortunate to obtain prints of some old pictures of Sakhalin Ainu, many of which were taken of the east coast. Therefore, some of the pictures in the book include Sakhalin Ainu from other regions.

2 / Subsistence economic activities

The Ainu settlements on the northwest coast of southern Sakhalin are very small, consisting of from a few to about twenty houses. Their summer settlements are located very close to the sea, while their winter settlements lie somewhat more toward the interior but still relatively close to the shore. In either case, the Ainu settlements are sandwiched between the mountains on one side and the sea on the other. Since in Sakhalin the mountain chain runs north and south in the center of the island, the mountains lie to the east of the settlements on the west coast. A schematic drawing of most of the settlements on the northwest coast in relation to surrounding nature is presented in Figure 2.

During the long snowbound winters in Sakhalin, Ainu males concentrate on hunting both land and sea mammals, while the women stay at home and make an entire year's supply of clothing for the family. Summers in Sakhalin are short, and the men make the best of it by fishing as much as possible, not only for immediate consumption but for winter supply for both humans and dogs. Women too are busy helping the men dry and smoke fish, as well as collecting plants, much of which is also dried for winter use. The patterns of Ainu economic life, then, sharply contrast between winter and summer or, more properly from the Ainu point of view, between the cold and warm season. The Ainu year starts with the cold season (for a detailed discussion of Ainu seasons, see Ohnuki-Tierney 1969a; 1973c).

ECONOMIC ACTIVITIES DURING THE COLD SEASON

Jobs for males during the cold season are hunting and trapping land and sea mammals, ice fishing, obtaining firewood, and carving tools at home. Women may do some ice fishing, but in the main their jobs are weaving, sewing, and embroidering at home. Storytelling beside the hearth is also an important as well as enjoyable part of winter life for the aged, the young, and even children. Some of the sacred stories recited by male elders take several nights to recount in their entirety.

For the Ainu the cold season starts when men go to the mountains for marten trapping (in mid- to late October in our calendar). When the hunters come back from marten trapping, the whole settlement celebrates a bear ceremony to which

16

many relatives and friends from various other settlements come. For those in smaller settlements, there almost always is a ceremony in a related settlement in which they participate. With a bear ceremony as a signal, the Ainu, until the turn of the century, then packed up and moved to their winter settlement farther inland.

Hunting and Trapping of Land Mammals Most of the hunting and trapping of land mammals takes place at the beginning and at the end of the cold season. At the beginning of the season, hunting guarantees tasty meat with much fat on it; the spring hunt procures meat of lower quality, so that it must be conducted before the animal fur changes to the less luxuriant summer coat. During mid-

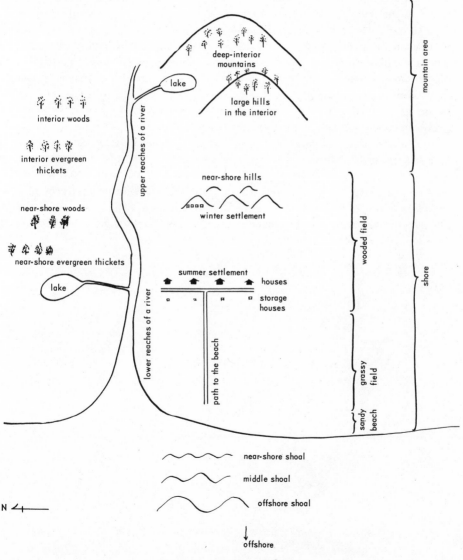

Figure 2. An Ainu settlement.

winter when the snow is too deep, hunting activities slow down. Important game animals include martens, bears, musk deer, reindeer, foxes, otters, hares, and squirrels. Wolves also were once eagerly sought for their tasty meat, although by the turn of the century they had retreated farther north and were no longer available on the northwest coast. Birds are not important hunting game, although some birds such as ptarmigans are shot, formerly with bow and arrow and more recently with a gun.

As noted earlier, marten trapping commemorates the beginning of the cold season. Men set off to the wooded area near the middle reaches of a small river and build temporary huts to stay in during the trapping. They place a log across the stream and construct on it a fencelike structure made of willow branches. In the center of the fence is a circular trap made of horsetail acquired from the Nanays through trade. The trap is constructed so that as a marten walks on the log and puts its head in the trap, the circular trap shuts on the neck of the animal. The men stay in the huts, every now and then checking on the traps. They may go back to their settlement temporarily for a bear ceremony if the weather permits a longer stay than usual, and therefore the bear ceremony must be held before the trapping season is over. Otherwise they stay on the marten trapping grounds until the stream freezes. They then take out the traps and go home.

For hunting larger animals, the Ainu use set trap bows. As an animal walks on a string connected to a trap, an arrow is released from the bow and the animal is shot. Although there is some information suggesting that the Sakhalin Ainu used to coat arrow tips with aconite poison, the Sakhalin Ainu in the recent past, including those on the northwest coast, all deny knowledge of the use of poisoned arrows; poisoned arrows were frequently used by the Hokkaido Ainu who eagerly

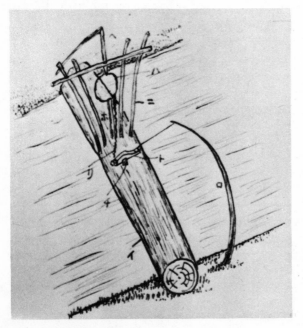

A marten trap. (Line drawing by T. Yamamoto)

sought "potent" aconite roots. Depending upon the size of the animals, the Ainu of the northwest coast made set trap bows in different sizes and placed them in the areas where each species of animals abounds. Recorded information indicates that the Ainu used to build huts to stay over temporarily for the hunting of these animals, although during the first half of the twentieth century marten trapping was the primary occasion when the Ainu used temporary huts.

Bear (*Ursus arctos collaris*) is the most important game hunted in this manner. Although the Ainu also hunt bears at the beginning of the cold season, they particularly seek the bears at the end of the cold season when the animals are either still in the den or have just left it. After the long hibernation, the bears are not as vigorous as they are later. The hunters may disturb a bear in its den until the animal comes out. Then they kill the bear right in front of the den, first with a bow and arrow and, if not successful, with a spear or knife. More often the hunters catch the animal shortly after it has come out of hibernation. At that time the bears go where their favorite plants are, since there are yet no fish in the rivers. Since their tracks are easy to trace in the spring snow, it is easy for the hunters to set a trap bow at an appropriate place. Hunting is least dangerous at this time since the grass is not tall enough to hide the bears.

At the end of the cold season bear and fox cubs are also eagerly sought. The Ainu raise them for the bear and fox ceremonies (Chapter 6).

Besides set trap bows, the Ainu also use simple circular traps to catch hares. While all other hunting and trapping are forbidden to women, they are allowed to trap hares. During the cold season, otters are caught with a bow and arrow through an ice hole, while they are trapped in rivers during the warm season.

Although set trap bows are the major hunting-trapping gear, the Ainu also use hand bow and arrow. It may be that the Ainu are the only people who use bow and arrow to hunt such formidable game as bears. The bow is about four to five feet long and is made of an evonymus tree around which strips of birchbark are sometimes, but not always, wrapped. The cord for the bow is made of nettle fiber, and when not in use it is taken off the stem. The shaft of an arrow is usually made of larch, and three pieces of eagle feathers are attached to one end with glue made from the skin of *činay* trout and nettle fiber thread. Imported metal arrowheads were used in the recent past, although information in oral tradition indicates that the Ainu once used obsidian and flint arrowheads, which then were replaced by bone implements.

Spears are a less significant weapon to the Ainu. They obtain spears through trade from the Nanays or from the Japanese. But during ordinary hunting, they are willing to use spears only after an animal is wounded by an arrow. There is no evidence that spears were among the repertoire of traditional hunting gear. They also use some male dogs in hunting, although not as extensively as some of the Hokkaido Ainu do, since the Sakhalin Ainu use set trap bows as primary hunting gear and dogs are used principally for pulling sleds.

The Ainu make multiple use of the animals they hunt. Of foremost importance is meat. They eat bears, foxes, wolves, martens, reindeer, musk deer, otters, hares, and squirrels. They are good meat eaters who relish biting off huge hunks of meat from the bones and who prefer animal meat in the fall when it is tasty and rich with fat. Another important use of the animals is for their fat. Bears, reindeer, and musk deer are major fat suppliers. When grease floats on top in a pan while the meat is being cooked, it is removed from the pan and stored in a seal stomach. The grease is used in cooking in general as well as for dip for dried fish in winter. It is also used as medicine, being applied to burns and to affected spots on the head when one has the skin disease of the head called *ke:čima* in Ainu.

Characteristically, the Ainu make relatively little use of the furs and hides of these land animals; instead, they use sea mammal and dog skins and even fish skin extensively. In the first place, it is strictly taboo to keep bear hides. Together with bones, they have to be properly placed at a fixed location in the mountains which is collectively owned by a settlement (Chapter 6). The furs of marten and otter, too, are not used by the Ainu, although they are eagerly sought as valuables to trade with other peoples, as discussed in Chapter 1. The only hides which the Ainu use for themselves are those of reindeer, musk deer, and hares. Reindeer hides are used as spread bedding for adults to sleep on. Musk deer hides are used for spread bedding for children and as the membrane for drums used in shamanistic rites. Neither reindeer nor musk deer hide is very sturdy, and hence the Ainu must have a regular supply to replace torn ones. Hare hide is also not very strong, but the fur is used for hemming clothing. Hare fur, foxtails, and marten fur, which are not tradeable because of poor quality, are used for winter headgear.

It is the women's job to prepare these hides either for trade or for use. They skin the animals, spread the hides on wooden frames and tie them with nettle fiber thread, and dry them either outside or inside on the wall close to the ceiling. After they are dried, they scrape the interior side with a small knife to get rid of unnecessary fat and other elements. Then they rub this side with a cottonlike substance from the rotten part of a willow tree in order to absorb excess grease from the hides.

When hunters run out of dried tree roots to use as strings, they use the tendon of *tibialis posterior* of reindeer. Various parts of animals are dried and saved for medicinal purposes. After contact with the Japanese and Russians, they also boiled and dried the testicles of marten and musk deer, which these peoples obtained from the Ainu to use as folk medicine.

The English terms "hunting" and "trapping" unfortunately convey essentially only the economic nature of the activities. However, it is of foremost importance to recognize that the Ainu regard these activities as religious in nature. Or, even more precisely from the Ainu point of view, there is no demarcation between activities relating to the obtaining of animal meat and those dealing with the deities. Important game such as bears, wolves, and foxes are at the same time the deities of the Ainu. Furthermore, it is ultimately in the hands of the deities whether or not the Ainu obtain food; if the Ainu behave respectfully toward the deities, the latter will provide abundant food, while if the Ainu misbehave in the eyes of the deities, famine may be the punishment. Therefore, hunting means for the Ainu either getting meat of the deities themselves or getting meat as a result of favors from the deities. Thus, animal meat is not only food for the stomach but its presence is also reassuring to the soul.

The religious nature of Ainu hunting also explains why the Ainu attach such importance to bear hunting. Although a bear offers the largest amount of meat at one kill, the number of kills is limited. Among the Ainu who do not systematically organize the hunt as some of the Hokkaido Ainu do, bears are never caught in great number. An average northwest coast Ainu would taste bear meat only two or three times a year. Seal meat and fish are far more important sources of food. As we have just seen bearskins are never used by the Ainu themselves. Therefore, the Ainu emphasis on the bear must be understood in terms of the religious significance attached to the animal, which is the supreme deity in the Ainu pantheon. Indeed, only for this animal do the Ainu perform a rite for every kill.

Ainu hunting and trapping activities are regulated, therefore, by what we might call "religious" rules. Thus women are barred from all hunting-trapping activities except for trapping nondeified animals like hares, since during hunting one is dealing either directly or indirectly with deities. The taboo against women is based on the belief that the smell of menstrual and parturient blood is offensive to the deities. Since the smell is believed to stay in the women's clothing even after washing, they are forbidden to participate in all matters dealing with deities, which include religious rituals as well as hunting of land and sea mammals. Likewise, a man who comes in contact with a parturient woman should abstain from hunting for several days; he is contaminated by the parturient blood, which is offensive to the deities.

Furthermore, every man at all times must go through a special purification rite when he goes up into the mountains for hunting, since the interior mountains are believed to be the habitat of all the deified land mammals and thus considered to be the most sacred part of the Ainu universe.

Another regulation requires that a hunter injured by a bear be treated respectfully as a bear deity until the injury is healed. Physical contact with a deity, namely, the bear, transforms the hunter temporarily into a deity. An injured hunter must not be placed in his home, but his family has to build a temporary hut next to the house. In the hut he is free from menstrual women or "unclean" firewood—firewood which has been lying outside and thus might have been contaminated by urine and other things that are offensive to the deities. If there is an elderly woman in the family, she must be in charge of the patient, using for cooking and warmth only clean, freshly cut firewood.

Verbal behavior too is regulated during the hunt. There are certain words that may not be used while a person is in the mountains. Instead euphemistic substitutes are used. For example, instead of using the term *tukara*, which is a word for seals, one has to use the word *sinuye*, which in ordinary circumstances means tattoo. The words which are affected by this regulation are either related to the sea or to foreign objects and foreign people; to the Ainu, foreigners reside offshore.

There also are some practical rules of thumb in hunting. For example, hunters must not sing or play any musical instruments, since bears are believed to be fond of good human voice or good music. Upon hearing them, they might come out and attack the humans. Since certain berries, roots, and grasses are favorites of both bears and the Ainu, women who gather these plants in the wooded areas should also observe this taboo; bears also frequent these woods in search of food.

Ainu hunters, like hunters in many other cultures, delight in telling stories about their hunting excursions, which constitute an exclusively male world. Here are two stories about a bear and two about lynxes. The first is a story about a clay-clad bear that is told by marten hunters, perhaps to remind the audience of the possible danger bears inflict upon men.

It is said that in the mountains are some extraordinarily large bears which spread clay over their bodies. They come out only at night. Each has a wild duck as a messenger who seeks out humans. Upon spotting humans, the duck reports to his master, who will come to attack them immediately. Unless, however, a wild duck assists in locating men, the bear is too lazy to search for them. Therefore, hunters should catch a wild duck as soon as they notice it, twist its neck, and sit on it.

The hunters should also flee as soon as they hear a pounding noise, since that is the sound of one of these bears covering himself with clay. At the same time, they should always be prepared with a large amount of clay, a spear, and a sharp wooden skewer in case a clay-clad bear happens to come to their hut. The bear would look like a huge bundle of clay with an opening only at its mouth. It will come beside the hearth or a bonfire outside and start drying its clay. The men should then keep adding more clay, making sure to cover the eyes, for as soon as the clay over the eyes falls off, the bear can see them and will attack the men. Meanwhile, the men should take the clay off the bear's armpits and the anus. While one man holds a skewer pointing toward the anus, the other two should immediately stab the bear in both armpits with spears. The bear will fall down on its rear end and the skewer will enter its anus. This is the only way that men can kill a bear of this kind and escape its attack. Hunters also should be very careful not to talk about these bears out loud while in the mountains, since they will immediately attack the hunters upon hearing them talk.

The other story about a bear depicts the animal-deity as a more friendly figure toward men.

Once a hunter lost his way and went by mistake into a bear's den. The bear welcomed the hunter and taught him how to lick his palms in order to quench his thirst and hunger. It explained that as the bears go up a river toward their dens, they eat and drink as much as they can. Then they can survive winter by sucking their paws. The hunter stayed in the den with the bear until spring when the bear led the way out of the den. The mountain snow was still deep, and every now and then the bear put the hunter on its back when the snow was too deep for him to walk. The two traveled for a long time until they came near the shore where the man's settlement was located. The hunter thanked the bear and told it to go back to the mountains before his fellowmen came to attack the bear.

Parenthetically I might add that I was fascinated by this story, because an almost identical "sucking paw" story has been reported to exist among the Hokkaido Ainu and Kurile Ainu. Furthermore, a "sucking paw" theme of a similar nature is also reported to be found among such peoples as the Lapps, Kamchadals, and some American Indian tribes, all of whom have elaborate rituals and beliefs about bears. (For further discussion of this subject, see Hallowell 1926:27–31.)

The third story concerns lynxes and is also told by marten hunters. The story centers on the Ainu belief that a lynx can either multiply or reduce its number instantaneously.

It is said that if a marten hunter encounters a lynx in the mountains, he should immediately climb a tall tree. He should first remove the rope which a hunter uses to tie his load on his back and make a knot at the end. He then should move this rope up and down from his perch at the top of the tree. As he lowers the knot at the end of the rope, the lynxes, having by then multiplied into hundreds, will all try to jump for it at the same time. Falling back, they will land on top of each other. Each will think that it is the man on the top of the tree who has fallen down, and they will eat each other. When this process has been repeated a few times, the few that remain will suddenly fuse into one and leave. If the hunter who has climbed a tree does not use this method to deal with the multiplying lynxes, the hundreds of animals will dig up the root of the tree so that it falls and then consume the hunter instead of themselves.

Another way of destroying a lynx relates to the animal's fear of water.

A hunter in the mountains should always carry a long pole. When he sees a lynx, he should go to a log bridge over a river where his marten traps are set, taking with him this long pole. Although the lynx may have multiplied by then, none of the animals will dare to cross the log bridge, since they are afraid of water. The hunter, standing on the center of the bridge, should swing his long pole in an attempt to hit the lynxes. Even a slight touch will hurt them and they will start to limp. If one is hit hard, it will fall into the river and drown. When they are sufficiently reduced in number, they will again become one and leave the area permanently.

Sea Mammal Hunting Of all the sea mammals, harbor seals (*Phoca vitualis*) are by far the most important game. Sea lions (*Eumetopias jubita*) are next in importance, and all the other available sea mammals are caught and used, although they do not constitute specific objects of hunt and are caught only when available. Whaling is not practiced among this group of Ainu, although whale meat is enjoyed on the rare occasions when a dead whale washes ashore.

When available, sea mammals are caught year round, although seal hunting at the end of the cold season constitutes the most intensive sea mammal hunting of the Ainu. At the end of the cold season, or in early spring in our sense, many seals gather on drift ice to give birth to their young. The Ainu start their seal-hunting trip before dawn and head for wherever drift ice is found; thus those in the southern parts of the northwest coast often go farther north, almost up to the former Russo-Japanese border. They use five-man boats and hunt for seals until after dark. Seal hunting on drift ice is the only Ainu activity in which the Ainu go beyond the near-shore area if necessary, while all their fishing activities are carried out in rivers, lakes, and near-shore sea. Before the introduction of guns, the Ainu used clubs and harpoons, especially the latter for seals whose senses are keen. They originally used barbed toggle harpoonheads made of bone and tipped with stone arrowhead, which were later replaced by imported metal harpoonheads. In the recent past, guns became the primary hunting weapon. In the case of harbor seals, the whole animal was brought back to the settlement in the boat. Sea lions are too large to carry back intact, and they are first cut up and the bones and some of the intestines thrown away. During the summer and fall the Ainu catch sea mammals as they come up on the shore, although the yield often is only a few in number.

The Ainu waste scarcely any part of the sea mammals, which constitute a highly important source of food, skin material, and oil. Not only do the Ainu relish sea mammal meat, they also enjoy the brain. Although for immediate consumption they cook the meat and the brain in sea water, some of the meat is preserved for winter supply. They make incisions in large hunks of meat, dry them outside for a while, and then smoke them over the hearth in the house. To extract oil, the thick layer of sea lion blubber and the thin layer of seal blubber are first boiled outside the house in a large pan. When it cools the melted fat is stored in containers made of either a seal stomach or the esophagus tube of a sea lion. The fat of seals and sea lions is used as dip for dried fish or as cooking oil. It is taboo, however, to use seal oil for lamp fuel.

Sealskins constitute a vital supply of material for garments and shoes. The women first remove the fat from the skin, beat the skin with a stick, and then step on the skin with their feet. They then add a spongelike substance from the rotten part of a tree trunk, wrap it up with the skin, and squeeze the bundle with their hands in order to absorb oil from the skin. They then shake the skin and hit it with a stick to get rid of the spongelike substance from the tree. Lastly they stretch the skin between two poles to dry. The skins are then made not only into garments and shoes but also into such items as bags and knife sheaths. Long leather strips made from baby seals are also important. Baby sealskin is chosen for the soles of sealskin shoes.

Like land mammal hunting, sea mammal hunting too is a religious activity, since the sea is the sacred residence of the sea deities and the sea mammals are the product of a sea deity, although they are not deities. As in the case of hunting on land, women are forbidden to participate in sea mammal hunting and sea fishing. This taboo, observed at the *Hurooči* and *Rayčiska* settlements, however, is not enforced everywhere on the northwest coast. For example, at *Ustomonaypo* women do go to sea and help men in rowing boats. Another taboo in sea mammal hunting is that hunters are not supposed to bring plants or food containing plants which the sea deities are believed to dislike. These include cow parsnip, bark of Japanese

A boat. (Courtesy of T. Yamamoto)

wych elm, and marsh marigold. It is even taboo to bring these plants to shore. There is no Ainu explanation as to why these plants are tabooed for sea deities. As in the hunting in the mountains, there are certain words which have to be euphemistically replaced. In sea mammal hunting, the words which require replacements denote either phenomena related to the sea, such as "boat" or "to row," or human beings, such as "man," "woman," and "human excreta."

As in the case of land mammal hunting, sea mammal hunting too gives rise to many exciting stories. For sea mammal hunting, the men go even beyond the Ainu land, if and when they meet storms. The following is a story told by a sea lion hunter.

Once upon a time some Sakhalin Ainu elders met fog and strong wind during their sea mammal hunting. They drifted to an island where there was an Ainu settlement. The settlement, however, was occupied exclusively by women, who, upon seeing the men, scrambled with one another in their eagerness to sleep with the men. These women were very dangerous, since they had teeth in their vagina and it could be fatal to sleep with them. One of the elders, however, was clever enough to insert his sword at the time of intercourse, thereby escaping his death and instead crushing her teeth. He safely came back to his settlement and told the story. These women are believed to expose their buttocks to the wind from the mountains and thereby conceive children.

For the Ainu who do not have a port and sail in a small wooden boat housing only five men, the wind which blows from the direction of the mountains is a sign of danger. On the northwest coast this wind will blow directly toward a boat approaching the shore and prevent it from going back safely to the settlement. Thus, the women in the story symbolically represent the threat of death and the story depicts the life-death struggle of Ainu hunters.

Ice Fishing   An additional supply of food during the frozen winter comes from ice fishing on rivers and lakes. Except for a large lake such as the one in *Rayčiska* where ice fishing may be done throughout the winter, it is done elsewhere only at the beginning of the cold season until around November and again at the end, starting around March. During midwinter the ice is more than two feet thick and fishing is not possible. Although ice fishing is theoretically a male job, it is in fact done often by women and children, since the men are usually too busy hunting during the ice-fishing season. They catch such fish as minnows, *tukusis* trout, Hucho trout, *hemoy* trout, salmon, *arakoy* smelt, *nokanceh* smelt, stickleback, and Wachna cod.

The Ainu use two methods for ice fishing. The one more frequently used is line fishing through an ice hole. They first make several holes about 8 inches in diameter and fish through these holes with a piece of red material as bait. Eventually they choose one which guarantees the best catch. At the end of the day, these holes are covered with snow so that they will not freeze overnight and thus be ready to use the next day. The other method is net fishing. A man puts up a net under the ice through several square holes made in the ice at set intervals. Women often take over and check the net every two to five days, depending upon the catch. This method was particularly successful at a river called *Tonkonay* near the *Notoro* settlement.

ECONOMIC ACTIVITIES DURING THE WARM SEASON

In contrast to heavy reliance on the mountains during the cold season, Ainu summer life revolves around water for fishing and grassy and wooded fields for plant gathering. The Ainu fish in near-shore waters, rivers, and lakes, but they rely more heavily on the latter two.

Fishing   The beginning of the warm season is signaled by the herring run, for which the Ainu used to move from their winter to summer settlement during the waxing moon of May. Even after the Ainu discontinued the seasonal movement, if their settlement is not located at a good place for herring, they often move to another settlement where the herring run is good. Early May in Sakhalin is still quite cold—in fact, the Ainu often interpret spring snowfall as a sign for the herring run. After a long frozen winter, they cannot miss herring fishing, although moving to an appropriate location for herring is not an easy task. For example, when Husko's father was still small, his family was caught in a snowstorm during the moving, and a newborn baby, to whom they had not yet given a name, caught pneumonia and subsequently died.

After herring fishing, the second major fishing at sea is *hemoy* trout from June until mid-July. The Ainu then shift their fishing ground to rivers and lakes. They follow the trout to a river and spear them as the fish gather at spawning ground in the shallows. Salmon is another important fish for the Ainu. Salmon fishing at its spawning ground in rivers marks the end of regular fishing in rivers and lakes.

Although herring, trout, and salmon constitute the most important fish, others are also eagerly sought when available, including Hucho trout, *tukusis* trout, minnow, flatfish, sculpin, *arakoy* smelt, codfish, and *hačuhčeh*. Of less importance are small fish—agreenling, *so:pukuna*, *činkoy*, and muddler—which gather under rocks in the shallows near the shore. Women simply scoop up these fish with their hands or with a basket. Shrimp, octopus, crab, shellfish, sea urchin, and other marine animals are used but are of much less importance to the Ainu. In the main the Ainu are efficient in concentrating their effort on large-sized fish which provide the maximum return for their effort and make use of smaller fish, shellfish, and other marine resources only as they are readily available.

There are a few kinds of fish which the Ainu avoid. The only really tabooed fish, however, is lamprey, which they call "bad fish" and abhor. The morphological resemblance of this fish to snakes, the most disliked animal of the Ainu, seems to be the explanation for this taboo. Although not a strict taboo, the Ainu ordinarily do not eat skate because of a story connected with the fish. Once an Ainu fellow had sexual relations with a skate because of the resemblance of the sexual organ of the fish to that of a human female. The union resulted in a good-looking boy who a number of years later visited his human father to announce his identity. Because of this legend, the Ainu do not eat the fish. They also avoid cutlassfish because of a belief that if one handles the fish his hands will become weak and powerless. Without a specific reason, the Ainu also do not ordinarily eat shark meat, although they extract oil from the liver of the fish.

In their near-shore sea, river, and lake fishing, the Ainu use a variety of equipment: net, net and boat, hook and line, spear, and basket trap. Above all the Ainu emphasize fishing for large fish with spears. Fish spears have a detachable hook which toggles as it goes into a fish. Basket traps are also frequently used. The flow of a river is blocked with a wattle fence which is open only in the center, where a willow basket, conical in shape, is attached to catch the fish. This technique is used for a variety of fish such as trout, *tukusis* trout, Hucho trout, and minnow.

Another type of fishing, of which the Ainu speak with great enthusiasm, is spear fishing by torchlight at night. Depending on the size of the vessel, three to ten people fish from a boat around the rocks in the shallows near the shore. Dried birch-bark bundles are used for torches. During this period the men fish at night until dawn and sleep in the mornings, leaving the job of drying fish entirely up to women. With this method they catch *hemoy* trout, Hucho trout, and sculpin. A welcome by-product of torch fishing is the catching of cormorants, which are attracted by the torch and fall victim. Cormorants are one of a few birds which the Ainu treasure for their meat.

The task of making the winter supply of dried fish is as important a job in the summer as fishing itself. Since hunting does not always provide sufficient food during the winter, the Ainu dry and smoke fish to carry themselves as well as their sled dogs through the long winter. They may dry fish whole, but the most frequently used drying method is to slice fish either in half along the backbone or into five pieces. In the latter case the center piece, being the backbone with little meat around it, is fed to dogs. The pieces are dried on wooden racks in a hut made especially for this purpose. Trout, salmon, flatfish, and codfish are all preserved this way. Men and women as well as children participate in the task of drying fish, although often the major responsibility goes to women since men are usually busy fishing.

The process of smoking fish from mid-August until mid-September is not simply a hard task but an enjoyable occasion for the Ainu, especially for young men and women. At this time, leaving children and the aged behind at home, men and women from several adjacent settlements gather in a wooded area near the upstream of a river. They build one hut for themselves and another without walls for smoking *hemoy* trout. Here they catch and smoke trout which have finished spawning. These fish are thin but less oily and hence better for preservation. Although the fire for smoking is kept going day and night and someone has to attend it, the rest of the people delight in taking off, whenever possible, to nearby woods to gather various kinds of berries. During this pleasant atmosphere romances often start, and many of the participants go back home with much to remember and talk about.

The fish provides not only food but also oil for cooking and other uses. Herring oil is especially treasured. The Ainu place many herring in a pot and cook them outside the house until the foam disappears from the top. The oil which floats to the surface of the pan is placed in a wooden box and cooled overnight. The oil is transferred to a bag made from a seal's stomach to be stored for the winter. It is used both for cooking and in their lamps. The herring from which oil is extracted is fed to the dogs. The Ainu also extract oil from the livers of codfish and shark by first slicing and then cooking them. This oil is also used for cooking.

Fish is an important source of material for garments, shoes, and bags (Chapter 3). Fish parts are also used as medicine. For example, when someone gets a boil on his tongue, a dried tongue of codfish is soaked in water and the water applied to the tongue and around the throat. For medicinal uses, the Ainu carefully store away various parts of a variety of fish.

The Ainu stress the importance of fish by asserting that fish is the food not only for humans and dogs but also for sea and mountain deities, namely, sea and land mammals. Despite the heavy reliance on fish as the source of food, oil, and clothing, however, the Ainu do not deify fish; fish are the product of a sea deity called *Čepehte Kamuy* (Chapter 6).

The Ainu make a significant distinction between lake and river fishing and fishing in the sea. In lakes and rivers, women are allowed to fish, even from boats. However, as noted earlier, women are strictly tabooed from fishing in the sea, where the sea deities are believed to reside. Consequently, women seem to feel closer to lakes and rivers. They point out that lakes and rivers are reassuring, since even when men are away on hunting expeditions they themselves can fish there without worrying about lack of food.

The Ainu attitude toward fish is one of familiarity. Since even children have an intimate knowledge of the behavior of fish, when a child overeats, an adult may reprimand him and say that his stomach will break open like that of a sculpin. Every May they observe that when the *hačuhčeh* run starts, sculpins come after them close to the shore where they devour the *hačuhčeh* and some die from overeating. Similarly, the Ainu make sure that a dead person may continue to fish, and will not lack this important source of food, by putting a few pieces of fishnet in the coffin. Since the dead Ainu is believed to resume his life just as he did in the world of the living, he is thought to continue fishing with the fishnet. Not only do the Ainu admire the beauty of fishskin and make it into garments, they believe that it was the design pattern on the *tukusis* trout which suggested the custom of tattooing women. This is explained in a short story in which *tukusis* trout appear as women wearing tattooes around their lips and weaving beautiful mats. The tattoo is a symbol of both female beauty and status in Ainu society. In this trout women story, too, we see the familiar place fish occupy in the life of the Ainu.

Plant Gathering   The Ainu of the northwest coast of southern Sakhalin never practiced horticulture or agriculture. (Although some Hokkaido Ainu are reported to have engaged in agriculture before the Japanese government enforced agriculture on all the Ainu, in both Hokkaido and Sakhalin, some consider that the Hokkaido Ainu agriculture may have been the result of diffusion of Japanese agriculture as early as the fifth century.)

The Ainu dependence on the plant world is as great as or greater than their dependence on the animal world. Therefore, plant gathering is an extremely important economic activity and is done primarily by women, although men are not tabooed from it. It is hardly an overstatement to say that an average adult woman knows practically every plant not only in the vicinity of her own settlement but in the adjacent settlements where she goes to gather certain plants which are not available closer to home. In settlements not favorably located for fish, plants become even more vital as food supply. Also, for families who do not have adult males to fish and hunt, a greater amount of plant food has to be obtained by the women of the family to supplement the shortage of fish and meat. For example, Husko remembers as a child that her mother worked extra hard to collect plants, often carrying her infants on her back. At *Hurooči* settlement, where Husko spent most of her maiden days, the fish supply was not abundant. Moreover, her father had several wives and would be away for extended periods of time visiting one of his spouses in another settlement. Therefore, Husko had to help her mother in plant gathering as soon as she could, and this is why her information on plants alone could result in a lengthy book. In this section, I shall give a bare outline of plant gathering.

Plant gathering starts with the digging of corydalis bulbs as soon as the snow melts. Ainu women use wooden digging sticks in order not to damage root crops. Even though corydalis bulbs are tastier in the fall, the women spend every spring day gathering these bulbs, since after a long winter this first root crop is a precious source of food for both humans and bear cubs if any are being raised. Corydalis roots are a favorite food of bears in the wild, although the Ainu cook them for their cubs. Except for immediate consumption, the rest of the roots are dried and stored for winter use. Later in the year when a bear ceremony is performed, corydalis roots serve as an important ingredient of dishes offered to the bear deities. Therefore, women will walk quite a distance to gather the roots if they are not available near their settlement.

The second major plant that is gathered is the leek, and this is done from July until mid-August. The Ainu cherish the flavor of the leek, and minced leek is an indispensable ingredient in most of their dishes. Furthermore, dried leek must be used during shamanistic rites. Also, its potency is believed to work in curing gynecological diseases. The Ainu carefully dig the plants out with digging sticks, so that the white bulb, which is even more delicious than the green leaves, will not be destroyed. Since large amounts of leeks must be gathered, dried, and stored away for winter, the Ainu spend many days gathering these plants. Men too participate when the weather is inclement for fishing. Since leeks often grow in grassy fields near the upper reaches of a river, two to three boatfuls of men and women may leave their settlement early in the morning, go up the river to gather, and come back in the evening. While gathering leeks, they often set a net in the shallows of the river near the leek field and cook the fish caught in the net for lunch. Perhaps because of the religious use of the leek, at the time of leek gathering the Ainu must perform a simple rite of offering at the end of the day. As they are leaving the field, each individual must take a few leeks, fold them in three, and cast them away one by one in different directions as offerings to mountain deities. If they have gone to gather across a lake or along the shore in a boat, then they must also perform the rite as they take off in the boat—this time in respect to the sea deities.

As soon as the leek season is over women busy themselves gathering other roots: Kamchatka lily during the latter part of August and bulbs of another plant in the lily family, called *kiw*, from late August to September. The gathering of Kamchatka lily bulbs is a big enterprise for the Ainu, although it is also a fun time, as in the case of trout smoking discussed earlier. There is an extremely good lily field at a place called *Oronnaypo* on the northwest coast. Thus, women from several different settlements, accompanied by men who can take off from fishing, come to this field. There used to be a small settlement there, but during Husko's time there were only two families there who jointly occupied one house. People from different settlements would stay in the empty houses as long as ten days or so, or until they had enough lily bulbs for the entire year. Since young men and women from different settlements gathered together, it was an enjoyable period for all. When Japanese fishing camps later penetrated into the area, Japanese fishermen visited them in the evenings.

August and September are the months for picking various berries, and this activity continues until after the first snowfall. The Ainu use about sixteen species of berries, all in cooking. Thus berries, too, are gathered in great quantity, and most of them are dried and stored for winter.

While continuing to gather root crops, berries, and other edible and medicinal plants, one of the most important activities around the time of the first snow is gathering of an urticaceous plant (nettle). Every day bundles of the plant stalk are gathered, and in the evening they have to be processed in order to make threads. The plant provides one of the major sources of clothing.

Besides the few mentioned above, the Ainu collect about one hundred species of edible and medicinal grasses and shrubs, in addition to berries, mushrooms, nuts, and marine plants. Next to food and material for clothing, medicinal use of plants comes third in importance for the Ainu. Other uses of plants, however, are of no less significance, meeting various needs in life. A few examples of interesting uses of plants will illustrate at least partially the encyclopedic knowledge which the Ainu have of plants and their uses.

During the summer the Ainu collect large amounts of such plants as cotton grass and store them. During winter they put these grasses in their shoes to keep their feet warm. Similarly, where we would be using tissue paper, toilet paper, and sanitary napkins, during summer the Ainu use the aromatic leaves of wormwood and chervil. During winter they use shredded stems of Rosaceae plants or willow for the same purposes. When there is an infant in the family, they collect the rotten part of tree trunks of willow and other trees, which has become a spongelike substance, and make it into powder by rubbing and crushing it with their hands. The powder is then placed in a diaper made of puppy or hare hide. Similarly, the rotten part of a birch tree is made into powdered form and used as a starter for fire making. In building houses and storage houses, they use bog mosses or lichen for chinking. Tree roots are dried and used as strings in making boats. The leaves of Rosaceae plants and a Ledum plant are gathered to brew tea. Cow parsnip, gathered and dried in summer and bleached on snow in winter, has a sweet white powder on it and the Ainu use it in cooking or simply chew on it as a sweet. There is a plant called *oyakema tanne* whose leaves are good to smoke, and Indian plantain provides a good blade to make beautiful whistling sounds.

The Ainu are also well informed about the favorite plants of animals. For example, they know the plants which bears like to eat and hence are very careful in areas where these plants grow. The Ainu use resin on cuts and boils, a practice they claim they learned by observing wounded bears rubbing their bodies against the resin on a tree.

It is no wonder that Husko often said that the Ainu had a perfect life, without having to rely on such "modern conveniences" as tissue paper and Chinese or Japanese material for clothing.

Despite heavy dependence on plants, basically the Ainu consider plants to be immobile and powerless, and hence do not deify them. Instead, they allocate the reign over plants to the deities in each spatial division of the universe where the plants grow. Thus the Ainu pay due respect to the mountain deities, for example, when they are gathering plants in the mountains. This attitude of the northwest coast Ainu toward plants again contrasts with that of other Ainu, both in Hokkaido and Sakhalin, who are reported to deify plants (Chapter 6).

A most interesting aspect of the Ainu plant world is that an Ainu term is a label for a certain part of a plant, be it its root, stalk, or leaves, and the rest is left unnamed. Thus, the Ainu term *hah* means the bulb of the Kamchatka lily, which like garlic consists of layers of petals. The term does not include other parts of the plant. Furthermore, the petals are classified into two kinds—smaller petals called *hahpi* and larger petals called *hahkite*. For drying the petals for winter use, the Ainu process these two kinds of petals separately and differently, hence the different designations. Different parts of some plants are used for different purposes. Then the Ainu give separate designations for different parts of the same plant. Thus the stalk of butterbur, which is cooked and eaten, is called *ruwekina*, while butterbur leaves are called *koriyam* and are used as rain gear or a cooking pot. The Ainu tie two or three leaves together at the root and use the structure as an umbrella. The heat-resistant and waterproof leaves of this plant are also used as a makeshift cooking pot; they fold several leaves into a conical shape and place root crops and other food in it to cook over the fire. Since the Ainu find little use for flowers of any plant, flowers are often left unnamed and receive little attention. Therefore, when the Ainu say that such and such a plant is "*pirika* (good looking)," it means that its useful part is well developed and in that sense good to look at; the term does not mean "beautiful" in our sense. The correct understanding of Ainu plant names first was pointed out by the late Professor Mashio Chiri, an Ainu and a superb linguist-anthropologist (for his life and his contributions to the study of the Ainu, see Ohnuki-Tierney 1973b).

3 / Daily life at home

This chapter deals with the daily life of the Ainu in and around the house, when the men are not hunting and fishing and when the women are not gathering plants. Our discussion starts with the description of the setting, that is, the Ainu house and surroundings. In every culture people give different values and meanings to different parts of their residence and the surroundings. More important, the members of the society in the main behave accordingly in each part. For example, even in American culture, in which metaphysical meanings of space are not emphasized, one does not receive a formal guest through a backdoor. Nor does a formal guest usually ask the location of the bathroom in front of company across the room in a regular volume of voice; the room itself has acquired certain meanings, as its various euphemistic designations indicate.

THE AINU HOUSE

All Ainu houses have only one room, but each section of the house and of the surroundings receives distinctive values which regulate Ainu behavior. Although the following discussion concentrates on the summer house and its immediate environment (Figure 3), about which more is known, the same general rules are applicable also to the winter semisubterranean houses which the Ainu discontinued using around the turn of the century, as noted earlier.

The ground rules for the Ainu are religious in nature and relate to the fact that the mountains are considered to be the most sacred part of the Ainu universe because this is where the mountain deities, including the bears, reside. Every house is therefore built with its sacred side toward the direction of the mountains. It is important to note that for the Ainu the "front" of the house is this sacred side; they make the sacred window on the wall on this side, and all the deities, that is, deified animals, are brought into the house through this window. Only the deities enter the Ainu house from the "front" and are seated, or "enshrined," on this side between the hearth and the wall. Of the human beings, only visiting male elders may sit here. To translate this Ainu direction into our more mechanical terms, the sacred side of an Ainu house faces east on the west coast of Sakhalin and west on the east coast.

Next in importance is the direction which corresponds to our north. This is

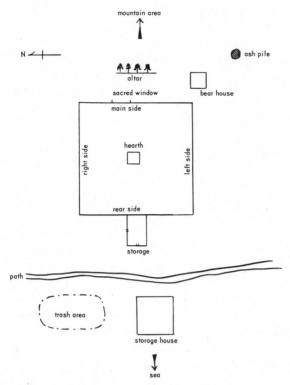

Figure 3. An Ainu house.

An Ainu settlement at Naipuchi on the east coast in 1906. As in all the Ainu settlements, a path runs between the Ainu houses (left) and storage area (right). In the rear a Russian log cabin is seen, indicating approaching outside influence (a Russian settlement on the right bank of the Naipuchi River). (Courtesy of T. Yamamoto)

where the master of the house and his wife are seated. It is called the right-hand side, or *si:monso:*. The Ainu picture a house as a body lying on its back with its head in the direction of the mountains and its right hand in the direction of our north. Like many, but not all, peoples of the world, the Ainu consider the right hand more sacred than or superior to the left, and this side of the house is referred to in Ainu as the right-hand side. In Ainu the word "right" also means "true."

Between these two most sacred directions lies the cardinal direction, corresponding to our northeast. Thus the sacred window is made on the wall of the sacred side toward the north. Also, ritual sticks for the God of the House are erected at the northeastern corner of the house, and those for the Grandmother Hearth (Fire Goddess) are placed at the northeastern corner of the hearth.

The sides corresponding to our south and west hold contrasting values. Thus, young males are seated on the south side of the house, while young females, who are held at the lowest position in Ainu society, sit on the west side of the house. The west side, facing the shore, is the "rear" side in contrast to the front side on the east.

These directional values are extended to the immediate surroundings of the Ainu house (Figure 3). Therefore, outside, at a short distance from the house, is the sacred altar, which is a fencelike structure adorned with ritual sticks with shavings. The Ainu perform all the group rituals at the altar. It is so sacred that everybody must walk quietly and speak softly when in that vicinity. The women are not allowed to traverse this area. Likewise, the bear cage and the ash pile from the hearth are located on the northeastern half of the area. Since the ash in the hearth seems to symbolize the Grandmother Hearth, the ash pile represents, so to speak, her sacred graveyard. Every now and then the Ainu ritually remove the old ash in the hearth and bring it out to the ash pile; this rite is considered to renew her life (Chapter 6).

In contrast, a more mundane character is assigned to the area south and west of the house. Thus the trash area is located to the west of the house across a

A wealthy man's house, with two hearths. (Drawing by T. Yamamoto under the supervision of an Ainu elder)

narrow path. The English term "trash," however, is misleading, since Ainu trash does not include much of what we consider trash, such as animal bones or broken objects. To the Ainu, bones of most beings of the universe represent the "body" of these beings. Without their proper treatment, the souls may not rest in peace and hence may cause trouble for the Ainu. Or the deified animals may not be reborn to visit the Ainu, that is, encounter them in the latter's hunt. Therefore, the bones of each "species" of being must be carefully placed in a proper place. Thus bear bones must be placed at a communally owned "altar" located in the mountains (see Chapter 6). Ainu trash includes only such items as the unusable parts of plants and pieces of wood left from woodworking. Indeed, this custom would certainly present a challenge for an archaeologist who aims at reconstruct-ing the total dietary habits of an Ainu group, let alone the entire culture.

In addition to being a trash area as the Ainu define the term "trash," the area west of the house also serves as an equivalent to a toilet for the Ainu, who do not build a special facility for the purpose. The women must be particularly careful in hiding grass soiled with their blood under the grasses in this area so that it does not get exposed to the Goddess of Sun and Moon, who otherwise would be offended. The Ainu meticulously observe this rule of conduct regarding the "trash" area, not so much because they themselves do not wish to be in contact with the "dirty" objects as because they believe that these objects are offensive to the deities and hence must be clearly separated from religious matters, which are placed on the north and east half of their immediate environment.

Human food also must be placed in the human section of the Ainu space. Thus, the aforementioned storage area is attached to the house on its west side, and a separate storage house built on stilts is located to the west of the house across a narrow path. The former, in addition to being the entrance to the house for humans, is the area in which are stored such objects as firewood, spare shoes, dried grass, and tools. During the winter the Ainu also keep female dogs and puppies here; male dogs are tied to the pole outside the storage house at all times. In the latter, the winter supply of food, such as dried and smoked fish, meat, and dried plants, is stored.

DAILY WORK

Just as the Ainu neatly assign different values and meanings to different sections of their spatial environment, they likewise divide their time. Thus, a day is divided into the "light-day" (daytime), which is assigned to human beings and the "dark-day" (night), which is allocated to the activities of deities and demons. The daytime is further divided, and all religious matters must take place in the morning, which runs from sunrise until the sun passes the meridian. During this time, the Goddess of Sun and Moon is in good spirits and therefore able to deliver Ainu messages to other deities. The Ainu day starts when sled dogs bark at sunrise. According to the Ainu, they also bark at noon and at the end of the day. During traditional times, the Ainu ate several meals a day, whenever they became hungry, although during the period described in this book they have adopted a three-meal-a-day schedule. Sled dogs serve as an alarm clock, not so much to signal the times for meals as to announce the divisions of the day which are of a religious nature and thus significantly affect Ainu activities.

Men's Jobs: Carving and the Care of Sled Dogs   When the weather is not suitable for hunting or fishing the men engage in such activities as obtaining firewood, doing various kinds of woodwork, and caring for the sled dogs. Metallurgy was not in the aboriginal repertoire of knowledge. Pottery was once made and used, but even the Ainu of the recent past do not remember its use.[1] Wood is the most extensively used natural material. The Ainu make objects out of wood, ranging from the largest boats and dwellings to the smallest utensils, using wooden nails and strings made either from the tree roots or strips of seal leather. Considered as the utmost in carving skill are the chains for decoration attached to the end of the handle of some objects such as chopsticks or spoons. Two or three extremely small chains are made from a single piece of wood or from a salmon canine.

The importance of the male role in woodwork must be further emphasized, since only males can carve religious objects; it is a strict taboo for women. Thus the men must carve out a great number of ritual sticks, which, being favored by all the deities, must be offered in all the rituals. Since they are sacred offerings, the men must carve them in the morning. Even the five-stringed musical instruments, called *tonkori*, must be made by males, since they are referred to as deities (see Chapter 6). Upon completion, the maker places a pebble in the hollow part, which is then regarded as the "soul" of the instrument. Then he adorns it with pieces of colored material and bells around its "neck." In Ainu culture art, religion, and other "aspects" are not compartmentalized, and much of the woodwork serves at the same time practical, aesthetic, and religious needs. The men take pride in producing beautiful forms as well as intricate designs incised on the products. Thus even a bowl or spoon, used daily by the Ainu, is a superb work of art. The Ainu point out that the ritual sticks are the favorite of the deities and are thus beautiful.

A gross misconception about Ainu carving must be pointed out here. With the tourist boom in Hokkaido, many Japanese have seen pictures of Ainu males carving bear figures, and many of these figures have been brought back by tourists. This phenomenon, however, is a result of acculturation, as is the use of bear skins for

---

[1] Besides wood, the Ainu once made and used stone and bone implements as well as pottery. During historic times, however, none of the Ainu in Hokkaido and Sakhalin even remembered the use of pottery. Furthermore, they all entertained the legend that once there were people on their land who were extremely small in stature and made the clay pots which the Ainu now find around their settlements. Ainu in several parts of Hokkaido and Sakhalin have told investigators that these small people were not their ancestors. The Ainu of the northwest coast of southern Sakhalin, however, claimed that they are their remote ancestors who lived in the beginning of the world. The lack of memory regarding the use of pottery, coupled with the legend about small people, once puzzled Ainu scholars who had been trying to decipher the identity of "enigmatic" Ainu; some claimed that there might have been another people on the Japanese archipelago prior to the Ainu arrival. However, Professor Torii, a Japanese archaeologist, learned during his visit in 1899 to the northern Kuriles that the recent ancestors of the Kurile Ainu used bone and stone implements and pottery and lived in semisubterranean houses. It is generally agreed among Ainu scholars that pottery was once used by all the Ainu but was replaced quite early in Sakhalin and Hokkaido by imported metal goods; it remained in use among the Kurile Ainu until the recent past.

trade purposes, mentioned in Chapter 2. In fact, the idea of bear carving came from Switzerland and was introduced to the Ainu in Asahikawa, Hokkaido, around 1920 by a Japanese in order for the Ainu to use their skill in carving to earn extra money. This practice has become widely diffused since then.

My inquiry into this matter started because Husko repeatedly stressed the taboos against using bear skins and carving bear figures. I had previously learned, however, that the Ainu in the recent past in practically all parts of Hokkaido and Sakhalin carved bears and released the bear skins to outsiders. This is another example which indicates that in many respects the northwest coast Ainu have retained their traditional way of life much longer than have other Ainu. Indeed,

An Ainu elder carving a ritual stick. (Courtesy of T. Yamamoto)

these taboos are more readily appreciated when we realize that bears are the most sacred beings in the Ainu universe. Such taboos are also in line with other religious taboos, such as the taboo against loudly pronouncing the names of their deities or keeping any physical representation of their deities in the home. The latter taboo caused the Ainu to quickly dispose of the Chinese garments with embroidered dragons which they acquired through trade; the dragons are one of the important deities of the sky. The only exception to this is a small bear head carved from a piece of wood which is used during a bear ceremony, and handed down from generation to generation. It is not so much a realistic representation of the bear head as a symbol of the deity.

Another important job for males is the care of sled dogs. Dog-drawn sleds are essential in the lives of the Sakhalin Ainu, providing the only means of transportation during the snowbound winter; the Hokkaido Ainu have never used them. Dogs are the only domesticated animal of the Ainu, unless one includes bear and fox cubs raised for ceremonies. They are also the only animals used for sacrifice during rituals; dogs must be sacrificed whenever a bear is killed, either during hunting or in a ceremony. As noted earlier, dogs are also essential as a source of food and clothing, for which only the female dogs and puppies are used, although strong female dogs may be used for the sled at times. Male dogs are carefully trained to be good sled dogs from the time they are small. Both adults and children enjoy watching puppies during practice, staggering and falling while pulling a sled. During this period the Ainu determine whether a dog is left- or right-shouldered. For a sled an equal number of left- and right-shouldered dogs are necessary. They also closely observe the dogs' temperament and intelligence so that each may be placed at the right spot in the team.

Ainu males perform two kinds of operations on male dogs. First, while a puppy, the dog's tail is cut off, due to a belief that energy which is needed for pulling the sled is wasted by the tail. The Ainu tie a piece of cloth and a string tightly around the tail next to the trunk and cut the tail off between two knuckles.

The other operation, castration, is done on a particularly warm summer day, since recovery of the dogs from the operation is thought to be quicker when it is warm. Also, the dogs have relatively little to do during summer. Unless the

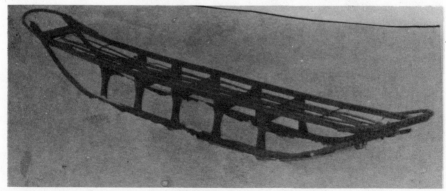

A sled. (Courtesy of T. Yamamoto)

operation is done skillfully, the dogs may die, and thus only a few men, usually older ones, are in charge of all the dogs. First they put a piece of wood in the dog's mouth and tie the dog's muzzle. Then an incision is made around the scrotum. When the testicles pop out they are cut off in a manner so that the tendons remain with the dog and no blood vessels are cut. There is, however, no ritual involved in this process and testicles are discarded on the road side. With an assistant to hold the dogs, a man can operate on many dogs in a day. When the dogs have minor bleeding as a result of either operation, the Ainu apply the resin of Yesso spruce on a strip of white birch bark and place it over the scar like a bandage, just as they do to a human scar. The castration too is believed to help save all of the dog's energy for pulling the sled at maximum capacity.

The Ainu exercise selective breeding, for which a leader dog is used. Hence in the case of a leader dog, they usually operate only on one side. Strong female dogs are saved for breeding purposes.

Depending on the size of the sled and distance of the trip, up to about fifteen of these carefully bred and trained dogs are fastened with a rope to a sled in alternating right and left fashion. The most important dog is the leader dog, the brightest but not necessarily the strongest of the team. When the snow is deep, as is often the case during the Sakhalin winter, the leader dog must sniff the ground under the deep snow in order not to lose the path. He does not merely take orders from the driver but may exercise his own discretion. Thus, when a sled trip is to begin and the leader dog refuses to start, the Ainu cancel the trip, taking the refusal as a sign that he senses dangers ahead of them, such as thin ice on the lake. There are two other dogs in the team with a special role: a second leader dog and the strongest dog, which is fastened closest to the sled. The sled dogs are always tied to a pole adorned with ritual sticks outside the house. They sleep directly on the ground or on a pile of grass during summer, or on fir branches during the winter.

Birch wood is used for the sled and the steer, and the rib bone of a whale is attached to the bottom of the sled as a runner. The total complex for sledding as a whole—the sled, dogs, and other necessary equipment—is called *nusu* in Ainu, and it is one of the most valuable properties of Ainu males, being handed down from father to son. The entire complex of *nusu*, however, is seldom owned by one person. More often, a chief of a settlement has the sled and several dogs, and an average member owns a few dogs and a small sled adequate only for short-distance travel. When a major trip is to take place, every household contributes its dogs and the whole effort becomes a community undertaking. A major trip must be planned well in advance. The day before the trip the women must cook dried fish with water made from snow and treat the dogs to them. During the trip, dogs are fed only dried fish and must not have any liquid, since the feeding of liquid during hard work is believed to cause stomach trouble. Just before starting, the dogs must be purified with a spruce branch whose tip is shredded into a ritual stick. The dogs, especially those in the front, are adorned with a colorful neckband and bells. Men wear a skirt-shaped sealskin garment for the sled riding and a covering over their thighs. The owner of the sled, often also the leader of the party, wears a special headgear made of two foxtails. At the time of the start, the leader of the party runs to the top of a hill or the highest spot in the community and signals for the rest of the members to gather with the sled and dogs, and the trip commences. The men mount sleds, wearing wooden skis with sealskin attached to the bottom. If necessary, the men can control the speed of the sled by their ski-clad feet, and at times they get off the sled and guide the dogs. It is indeed a spectacular event for the people in the community to watch the beautifully adorned men and dogs leave on a sled trip, while listening to the bells ringing in the cold crisp air. The return of the party from a trip is equally eventful in the mind of the people, and the women wait for their return with the food not only for the men but also for the dogs all prepared.

During the summer, the sled dogs have relatively little to do. However, when a load of goods must be transferred to a distant site, they are used to pull a boat along the sea or lake shore while a man steers. This is possible only when the shore is relatively devoid of rocks, and the water must be calm.

Women's Jobs: Sewing, Weaving, and Cooking   The women engage in numerous jobs at home which revolve primarily around feeding, clothing, and general care of the family. Here I shall describe cooking and making of garments, but will discuss child care in the next chapter in the context of the life cycle. Women are extremely busy during the cold season when men have relatively little to do. They have to prepare the entire supply of clothing for the year, which includes in this cold climate not only the various kinds of garments but also head- and footgear and gloves. Clothing is made from three kinds of material: plants (nettlelike plants, called *hay* in Ainu, and Japanese wych elm, called *ah* in Ainu); animal skins (primarily those of seal and dog); and fish skin. Birds' feathers were not used by the Sakhalin Ainu. The most treasured garment is called *tetarape*, which means "white thing" in Ainu, and is the most time-consuming to make. This garment is made exclusively from nettlelike plants (*Urtica Takedana* Ohwi), which are irritating when raw. Around the time of the first snow, sometime in October, women gather bundles of these plants, as noted earlier. At night, beside a lamp made from a shell which burns herring oil, they peel the outer skin with a shell of a bivalve called *pipa*. They twine the plants, dry them, and store them until January. Then they go through the long process of bleaching the fibers until they are pure white, first by soaking them in lukewarm water, repeatedly stepping on them in the snow, and finally hanging them on a pole to dry. The entire process of bleaching alone takes about two months. Then they must make thread from the fibers before they can begin to weave them into *tetarape*. Despite all the work involved, the Ainu women are eager to make fine *tetarape* for their elders, who alone are privileged to wear them. In areas such as *Hurooči*, however, where this plant is extremely abundant and the Japanese wych elm, another plant used for garments, is scarce, even younger men wore this garment.

Far less time-consuming as a plant material for garments is the fiber of the phloem found just inside the bark of the Japanese wych elm (*Ulmus laciniata* Mayr). Men, who are sometimes joined by women, go to the woods to peel the inner bark from the elm tree. Women soak it in salt water for about a week to ten days and then allow it to dry. By then each layer of the bark comes off like tissue paper and is ready to be woven into a garment called *ahrus*. Since the fiber from the elm is not as strong as the thread made of nettle, the nettle thread is

An eating utensil in the shape of a boat. (Courtesy of T. Yamamoto)

*A woman at Naipuchi in a sealskin garment making nettle
fiber thread. (Courtesy of T. Yamamoto)*

An east coast Ainu woman in a sealskin garment. (Courtesy of T. Yamamoto)

A fish skin garment (front and back) for women. (Courtesy of T. Yamamoto)

usually used as woof in weaving; elm is used as warp. Garments which are made primarily from the elm bark are worn by young males and females, but even elders wear them for daily use.

A winter garment called *ohko*, worn exclusively by women over an *ahrus*, is made of sealskin. Ainu women skillfully arrange white fur from the seal's stomach and black fur from the back to produce a beautiful design pattern. Sealskin is used also for men's and women's shoes. Another type of garment worn by men, women, and children is made of puppy skins, usually from female puppies about eight months old. The dog skin has an advantage over the skin of other animals such as fox in that it does not collect snow. As noted earlier, the use of bear skin is a strict religious taboo.

Another important source of material for garments, bags, and shoes is the skin of such large fish as salmon and three kinds of trout, called *hemoy*, *čiray*, and *tukusis* in Ainu. After cutting the head and the tail off, Ainu women dry the fish until the skin comes off easily. It takes about 40 to 50 adult fish to make a garment, which is worn by women on special occasions. Because of the importation of silk and cotton materials, the fish skin garment was the first to disappear from the aboriginal repertoire. Husko remembers only once seeing a woman clad in a beautiful fish skin garment for a bear ceremony and receiving the admiration of others. Fish skin bags met the same fate of early disappearance. Fish skin shoes, however, were used much longer. Since the beginning of the 1930s, the men have used Japanese rubber shoes for most occasions, but continued to use fish skin shoes for marten hunting; insulated with grass, these shoes were warm and did not freeze. Thus, the women considered the making of fish skin shoes as one of their most important jobs. They carefully dry the skin of the *čiray* trout. One large fish and twelve small ones are necessary to make a pair of boots.

Some of the garments are open fronted, while others have the so-called mandarin collar. The style of garment is the same for men, women, and children. As noted earlier, it is the material of the garment that indicates sex and status differences. For example, the nettle fiber garment is worn only by male elders. In addition, the amount of design and color used in the pattern of decoration also indicates these differences. Thus the male elders' garments must be adorned with many designs in which red must be abundantly used. The color red, which ranges from dark red and almost brown to bright red in our color schema, is produced by soaking the material in water in which the bark of alder has been placed; alder bark turns water red. Women's garments, in contrast, have only a small number of designs and no red. These designs, which are not only intricately beautiful but symbolically expressive of the owner's social position, are either woven in, appliquéd, or embroidered. There are basic units of designs and the women create their own configurations, applying them without paper models or line drawings.

The Ainu do not prepare special garments for special occasions. Even shamans do not have a special outfit, although on the east coast of Sakhalin shamans wear a special garment with elaborate paraphernalia, which is the result of influence from the Oroks and Gilyaks. For the bear ceremony, everyone saves a newly prepared garment, and this adds to the great feeling of anticipation for this most sacred and yet most enjoyable ceremony.

(Left) Nu:makisranke, an elder from the Rayčiska settlement on the northwest coast (circa 1940). He wears the prestigious garment made of nettle fiber, called tetarape in Ainu. (Courtesy of T. Yamamoto) (Below) Embroidery designs by Husko.

Basic patterns of design. (Courtesy of T. Yamamoto)

Nightwear, made slightly larger than daytime garments, is made of warm dogs' skins. For sleeping, the Ainu put grass on the raised platform next to the wall. They then put down mats and a reindeer skin for adults and musk deer skin for children. With warm nightwear they need no coverings over them. On extremely warm nights, they sleep on the grass field next to the shore, men on one side and women on the other. They consider this sleeping arrangement fun and seem to have a similar feeling as some of us do toward sleeping in a sleeping bag during camping.

Besides making clothing, the women must also weave mats from sedge grass. These mats have many uses. They are used not only for sleeping but rolled up they serve as pillows. They may be hung at the doorway as a windbreak or used as containers for swords and other treasures. The mats are used to sit on inside the house, since the Ainu do not use chairs. Mats are hung on the wall inside the house to prevent drafts, which is usually a common problem in the relatively crudely made houses on the coastal settlements where strong winds frequently blow across the Japan Sea. These wall mats also serve as interior decorations in the house and are used for the same purpose during rituals. For this purpose, the women weave colored designs in intricate patterns. These designs are made with colored strips of the inner bark of elm, which is also used, as discussed earlier, for garments. Red, the most important color for ritual occasions, is often abundantly used, and for this purpose the elm fibers are dyed in the water with alder bark, as mentioned before. For bright red Ainu women use the juice from crushed berries of the vacciniaceous family called *enonoka*. Black, which ranges from our gray to dark blue and black, is obtained from the juice of crushed *kurasno* berries. Yellow is made from the outermost bark of the cork tree, which, as in the preparation of the red dye, is soaked until the water turns yellow.

Cooking is another important activity for women, although participation in cooking by men is not regarded as taboo or effeminate. When the women are busy gathering plants, the men, especially the younger ones, do the cooking. Their method does not include sautéing, deep-frying, or roasting. By boiling and simmering, the Ainu cook their food thoroughly. They abhor raw meat, and the eating of it is confined to the ritual consumption of blood and brains during the bear ceremony. Among the Hokkaido Ainu, however, there is reportedly a more extensive use of raw food. The Ainu preference for well-cooked food is used as a reason for their dislike of neighboring peoples such as the Gilyaks, Oroks, and Japanese, all of whom follow the "barbaric" custom of eating raw food. (The Ainu dislike of these peoples is apparent considering their exploitation of the Ainu in the past. However, many peoples of the world choose such unimportant customs as eating habits to justify their prejudice. Thus, the Japanese, in turn, dislike the garlic and leek used by the Ainu, Chinese, and Koreans and thus justify their prejudice toward them.)

The Ainu diet varies greatly in the cold and warm seasons. During winter they have more land and sea mammal meat than during summer, although they must supplement their diet with a large amount of dried fish and plants in order to get through the lengthy winter. Their summer diet consists primarily of fresh fish and plants. Of the mammals they hunt, meat of the bear, reindeer, fox, otter, and seal is especially treasured, since it is rich with fat. Another important and favored source of meat is female dogs. Not many birds are eaten and some are even taboo to eat. However, such birds as sea gulls, crows, cormorants, and ptarmigans are well liked.

The ground rule of Ainu cooking is not to mix major ingredients. Thus not only meat, fish, and plants (except herbs) are cooked separately but each species of animal must constitute a separate dish. Meat is cooked with the bones still attached to it. Marrow is very popular. Meat is cooked in sea water with a spruce branch and a piece of kelp (seaweed). After Japanese influence reached the area, some Ainu cooked meat with the newly introduced potato. However, the taboo against mixing meat with other food has been observed strictly in regard to the bear; the meat of the supreme deity must not be contaminated by anything else.

The Ainu are connoisseurs of fish. As in the case of meat, they prefer the rich taste of fish in the fall to that in spring. They treasure the meat in the "cheek" and in the eye sockets, although they do not eat the eyeball as do some peoples. They also relish fish intestines. A potful of boiled fish intestines garnished with minced leek is a real treat for the Ainu. One of their favorite dishes is made from the skin of *čiray* trout. The skin is sliced and soaked in sea water and then cooked until the skin melts into a mushy substance, which is further pulverized in a wooden mortar with a pestle. After some berries, such as *enonoka* or *hu:tureh*, are added, the mixture is frozen into a gelatinous substance in a wooden container outside the house. It is then sliced and served. This favorite winter dish is one of the foods offered to the bear deities during a bear ceremony. Dried fish, either as is or soaked in water, is eaten with oil, especially that of the bear, as a dip. It also provides the standard menu for a carry-along lunch.

Plant food constitutes a dish on its own and is therefore cooked separately from the meat and fish. It is cooked with either seal or herring oil, and often mashed eggs or the milt of fish is added. When the main plant ingredient is a root crop, it is called *anasis*; roots are always cooked and mashed well. When the leaves and stalks of edible plants are the main ingredients of the dish, the dish is called "*čikaripe*." The Ainu consider a particular kind of clay flavorful and often use small amounts of it in these plant dishes. Berries too are often added in these dishes.

In addition to the rule of not mixing ingredients, the most important rule in Ainu dietary practice is that after the cooking, the bones of each species of animal and fish must be carried to their respective bone pile, as we have already seen.

There is another refreshing routine for women. During the summer the women start their day by going down to the edge of the grassfield next to the beach and surveying the shore. As in the case of plant gathering, their trained eyes can spot anything useful that is washed ashore, such as edible marine plants, shellfish, and other small marine animals. Occasionally they even find dead fish, a marine bird, or even a sea mammal which is still fresh and hence edible. In this northern land, the air in early morning on the shore is chilly and brisk, and many women consider the early morning walk to the shore enjoyable. Even the children learn how to spot useful objects on the shore, and later during the day they often find driftwood, empty shells, bottles, and other goods from strange lands, all of which become enjoyable toys. They also look for food. One day while I was talking with Husko, her ten-year-old grandson came running excitedly from the shore. He had in his hand a particular kind of sea gull, called *mas* in Ainu. The meat of this sizable marine bird provided an unexpected treat at the supper table. Furthermore, the bird would have supplied the best medicine for a dermatological disease of the head called *ke:čima* in Ainu, although at that time nobody needed it. When someone has *ke:čima*, after removing flesh of the bird for eating, they next remove the back, head, legs, and wings. They place the breast of the bird over the patient's head so that the layer of fat directly touches the affected parts of the head. If this is left on the head overnight, it is said to heal the head, which is then washed with water. After applying either herring oil or dog oil, the head is then wrapped with leaves of butterbur for a few days.

GAMES, MUSIC, DANCING, AND STORYTELLING

Besides the activities just discussed, which are all more or less related to practical matters, Ainu life is rich indeed in such activities as games, music, dancing, and storytelling. What the Ainu call *hečire* includes our games, sports, and several other kinds of nonpractical activities. A *hečire* can be as simple as tying grass at the roots during plant gathering. A person who plays this trick "gets a kick" out of watching those who come after him fall because of the tied grass. Several indoor games are played by both men and women, such as throwing a bunch of sticks into the air and catching an odd number of sticks (3, 5, 7 . . .). The one who catches the largest odd number of sticks wins. In these indoor games the winner is rewarded, often with dried fish, and the loser is penalized; penalty ranges from slapping of hands, marking of the face and other parts of the body with soot from the bottom of a pan, to various kinds of errands. An errand could be fetching cold water, when summer, from a distant spring, and the one being penalized may have to go through an area where bears are known to frequent. For these errands, however, the loser too receives a dried fish. A most popular game is a tug of war, which is played whenever there is leisure time. About ten people will decide to play this game, and it is announced to the people in the settlement who will start preparing dishes to treat them. They string several heads of either dried cod or herring at one end of a strip of sealskin and go around the settlement, visiting one house after another. At each house they throw in this strip with fish heads on it. As they throw it in, those in the house must immediately grab the end and start a tug of war with those outside. Sòmetimes when there are not enough people inside the house, some may quickly tie the string to a pillar or a leg of the raised platform for sleeping. At any rate, when the game is over the visitors are invited in for treats.

There are several outdoor games exclusively for males, especially the younger ones. These are more contests of male skills and courage than games, although the Ainu classify them in the general category of *hečire*. In these games the reward for a winner is the esteem of the people itself. Thus, the winner in one game is said to become a great leader in the future, in another a good seal hunter, in yet another the winner of many women, and so forth. The most daring contest is performed when a bear, which is being raised in the settlement, is removed from its cage in order to be taken to the river or seashore for bathing. Young men are encouraged, but not forced, to charge directly toward the bear, which is being restrained from the rear by a rope held by other men, grab his ears, and retreat immediately. If a man fails to grab the ears, the bear will grab him instead and perhaps harm him seriously. Or if the bear retreats just as he charges, the youth may fall in front of the bear and become its prey. If a man does this successfully, it is said that he will become a great leader in the future. Once during a bear ceremony Husko's husband, with the encouragement of his uncle, did this successfully. However, the two men were reprimanded by their elders, since a bear is believed to be much more powerful at the time of a ceremony than at ordinary times, and it is thought to be too dangerous to engage in this sport at that time. The increased power of the deity during the ceremony is believed to be derived from the numerous ritual sticks which the Ainu offer to the bear.

One of the most interesting aspects of the games and other activities discussed above is that the Ainu, who ordinarily stress mutual help rather than competition, express their skills and personality most spontaneously in these activities. Among the women, there are some like Husko who are too shy even to participate in these games, while others actively seek the opportunities. By the same token, some men are more eager than others to prove their valor and physical ability in the eyes of others. However, none of the Ainu games involve physical harm to the opponent, as in our boxing, or the one-to-one confrontation of our tennis and fencing. In the main, participants in Ainu games and sports do their best without direct reference to other participants.

Although not considered as a *hečire*, a favorite pastime is riddles. One example is a question, "What is that which without legs goes to six settlements setting traps, while the person with legs stays at home?" The answer is "a boat." In Ainu the number six expresses the concept of many. "The person with legs" is meant to be understood as a "storage house," which is the only Ainu structure built on stilts. Since parts of a building receive terms for human body parts, the stilts are referred to as legs. The Ainu have a fairly large repertoire of standard riddles such as this one and they enjoy questioning each other. These riddles often tell outsiders how the Ainu perceive things around them.

The Ainu love singing, playing musical instruments, and dancing. Their music has a tranquil beauty, and their dancing is characterized by graceful movements rather than rhythmic vigor. In fact, the Ainu often criticize the dancing of the Oroks, their neighbors, which involves more vigorous physical movements, as lacking in dignity and grace. Aside from the drum of the shamans, which the Ainu do not regard the same as other musical instruments, the most important in the Ainu view is the aforementioned five-stringed instrument called *tonkori*, which they refer to as a deity. Other musical instruments are a flutelike *pehkutu* and a *muhkun*. The latter is made of a small stick, a piece of split bamboo, and a string. Intricate music is produced by the player blowing through the bamboo piece while pulling the string at short and regular intervals. Each tune played with a *muhkun* tells a story of its own without accompaniment of words. One tune tells of a mother searching for her lost child in the snow, crying and falling down on the snow every now and then. Another tells about lovers who eloped. Although they had picked a meeting place, when the man arrived the woman was not there, perhaps having gone to another place by mistake. Thus the tune of the *muhkun* represents his voice saying, "If you hear this tune, please come to me." As in this case, musical instruments often serve as a means of communication between young lovers; the two would agree on a particular tune as a signal, and a man or a woman would call his or her love by playing this tune. There also are several kinds of songs such as love songs, lullabies, boat songs, and the like, of which the more famous ones have been handed down through generations.

Of all the nonpractical aspects of the Ainu life, oral literature is by far the most well developed, both among the Sakhalin and Hokkaido Ainu, who are extremely proud of their traditions. As noted earlier, their epic poems are regarded by scholars as comparable in their literary quality to the Greek epics. Fortunately, the high quality of Ainu oral literature caught the attention of many scholars and much of it has been recorded (see Chiri 1944; Kanenari 1959–1965; Kindaichi

Husko's tonkori *musical instrument, 1969. (Scale 5 cm)*

Husko playing the tonkori *(circa 1960). (Courtesy of Husko)*

Husko's muhkun *musical instrument, 1969. (Scale 5 cm)*

1944; Pilsudski 1912). It is particularly noteworthy that Matsu Kanenari, a brilliant Ainu woman, recorded five-volume epic poems by herself in subphonemic notation. She is an aunt of Professor Chiri, an Ainu scholar of the Ainu culture.

Ainu in each region have their own classification of their oral tradition, and an Ainu would specify to which genre in their classification a particular piece of literature belongs. The northwest coast Sakhalin Ainu classify their oral literature into four categories, which are, in order of importance, *hawki*, *oyna*, *učaskoma*, and *tuytah*. I must refer to these categories in Ainu terms, since the translation of them renders little of the nature of the stories in each category. The stories in the first two categories are epic poems and are called *sa:korope* ("things to sing"), since they must be told with *sa:kehe* ("melody," "singing"). Besides the two characteristics of being composed in verse and told in singing, there are a few other defining characteristics for a story to be included in one of the two categories. Thus the subject matter must deal with either deities or the Ainu culture hero *Yayresu:po*, who is believed to be a demigod. The setting of the story is at the beginning of the universe. Also, the language involved in these stories includes a great deal of what the Ainu call the language of the deities and the language of the aged. These are special sets of lexical and grammatical uses which are used exclusively by the aged and are considered greater than ordinary diction. The language of the deities in particular is used primarily in prayers, that is, in the communication of male elders to the deities. Furthermore, these stories are characteristically told in the first person singular. Thus a deity or the culture hero tells a story about himself, and the singer becomes the protagonist. Lastly, these poems include refrains throughout the entire composition. Many of these refrains, which always have beautiful resonance, have lost their original meaning and are no longer meaningful phrases. Others are onomatopoetic of the voice of the protagonist when the latter is an animal deity. Still others are meaningful phrases. Of the two categories of *hawki* and *oyna*, the former are considered to be the greater. Although both deal with deities and/or the culture hero, *hawki* involves battle scenes. Being the greatest of all stories, and involving the language of the deities, *hawki* must be told by male elders. Although *hawki* may be told on ordinary nights, it must be sung when someone is gravely ill or an epidemic is present.

The two other categories, *učaskoma* and *tuytah*, are composed in prose style, and the Ainu consider them as light stories. *Učaskoma* most often deals with the great chiefs, who are not "mythical" or "legendary" figures in the beginning of the universe but actual figures whom the Ainu consider to have lived some generations ago. The *tuytah* genre is made up of various fairy tales, including stories of non-deified animals who in some stories transform themselves into human form.

The oral tradition is an extremely rich source of information on Ainu culture, as illustrated by an *oyna* which Husko taught me (the entire story in Ainu with interlinear translation is published in Ohnuki-Tierney 1969b).

A story is told of the culture hero *Yayresu:po* and his guardian deity *Čiriki-yankuh*, who lived on an inner mountain behind the settlement where the culture hero was chief. The deity's daily routine was to come out of his house and put his chin on the lower edge of the roof (this is how the Ainu describe his great stature). He then looked toward the settlement to see if everything was all right. He also had a pair of birds—a husband bird of a golden color and a wife of a silver color. They were constantly on the lookout and cried noisily to inform the deity when they detected something wrong at *Yayresu:po*'s settlement.

One day the deity had a dream that some unidentified creatures were about to attack *Yayresu:po*'s settlement. He therefore made *Yayresu:po* sleep and dream, during which he told the culture hero about the arrival of the demons. The deity instructed the hero that when the demons asked their own identity, he should reply that they were the children of *tonkori* musical instruments; otherwise the demons would become angry and kill him and his people. The next day the birds cried noisily and the deity decided to go to *Yayresu:po*'s settlement. As he was descending the mountain, the deity was so large that short trees barely reached his ankle and tall trees reached only to his knee. As he walked his legs created a strong wind, causing the trees to swing back and forth. Looking at the horizon, he saw the typical fog of blood there (Ainu demons usually appear with a fog of blood). Then he went back to his mountain.

The scene now changes to *Yayresu:po,* who fell sound asleep immediately after the dream. He woke up early the next day and started the fire in the hearth. As he stepped outside, he saw a fog of blood forming on the horizon. Returning inside, he heard the voices of two demons who were coming up the path from the shore (there is always a narrow path connecting an Ainu settlement to the shore [see Figure 2]). They came to *Yayresu:po*'s house and began to talk even at the entrance (this is considered to be bad manners). They sat at the upper side of the house (where only male elders are invited to sit) and talked as though they had known *Yayresu:po* for a long time. When they asked about the identity of themselves, *Yayresu:po* replied that they were perhaps children of *tonkori* instruments. Upon his reply the demons disappeared instantly, and all that remained were two musical instruments lying on the upper side. *Yayresu:po* took them outside the house and broke them into pieces with an axe. Then he fed the pieces of the demon's bodies to all the trees, grass, and ground.

Since there is not enough space here to interpret this story in detail as ethnographic material, I shall discuss the three major themes. First, any Ainu listener would readily be reminded of an important taboo: upon moving, anyone who leaves behind a tool, a musical instrument, or any other object must break it into pieces. Otherwise the soul of the object would not be able to get out of the "body" to rest in peace in the world of the dead, and hence cause troubles for the Ainu. This taboo stems from an Ainu belief that most of the beings of the universe have a soul and upon death the soul should leave the dead body and go to the world of the dead. Thus the story illustrates what will happen if a careless Ainu forgets this basic courtesy to beings of the universe.

Second, the story fully depicts the Ainu notion of demons. Ainu demons represent the threat to the life of the Ainu, as symbolized by blood fog. Since demons mean death, the Ainu must make sure that demons do not reincarnate; hence, every demon story ends with the ritual of cutting the demons into pieces to be consumed by the beings of the universe.

Most important, the story illustrates the essence of the Ainu world view. Namely, the Ainu live in the universe in which the Ainu, their deities, and demons are the primary occupants. Although the threat of demons is real and to be expected at any time, the Ainu can live in peace with the protection of their deities, provided that the Ainu behave respectfully toward them. In the beginning of the world, the culture hero was the mediator in the communication between the deities and the Ainu, and this communication, then as well as now, is facilitated through dreams.

Some of the epic poems of *hawki* and *oyna* take two to three nights to complete. Thus they are told during long winter nights when the Ainu have relatively little to do. Outside it is bitter frozen winter in this northern land, but inside, beside the hearth, where all the stories are told, it is warm, especially when the Ainu were living in semisubterranean pit houses. A storyteller-singer, when it is a male elder, often falls on his back at the climax of a story and recites the story while waving his arms in the air. The epic thus dramatically imprints in the mind of the listeners the greatness and kindness of the deities in protecting the Ainu, and the sagacity and valor of their culture hero who combats with the demons. The occasion also enhances in the eyes of the young the deep knowledge of these storytellers, most of whom are aged.

4 / The life cycle

The Ainu distinguish between minors and adults, and both of these groups are further subdivided. The category of minors includes infants (*uhasinpe*, newly born, or *pon tennehpo*, babies) and youngsters, *hekači*. The adults are divided into young adults (*sukuh utah*) and "old adults" or the aged (*onneru utah*). This chapter traces the aging of the Ainu individual by describing rites of passage, beliefs, and behavioral expectations attached to the various stages of the life cycle.

BIRTH

Birth is considered to be an expression of favor of the deities, since the conception and birth of each human being is attributed to the deities in general and to a deity called *Aynu Sikahte Kamuy* in particular. The Ainu believe that human beings are not powerful enough to create a human life by themselves and that mere copulation does not result in a child. They desire as many children as possible, for in theory children are proof that their parents are on good terms with the deities. From a practical point of view, this belief reflects the keen awareness of the Ainu that in their old age they must depend upon their children for survival. Although natural resources were abundant during aboriginal times, especially with such a small number of people occupying the land, survival in this northern climate by hunting and gathering has always been extremely difficult, and the conditions of existence put a premium on physical strength. Thus, subsistence economic activities become increasingly hard to perform as one gets older. Furthermore, mutual help is essential in Ainu life, not only in such activities as obtaining food and building houses but also in emergencies such as fires. Therefore, every human being, be it one's own child or a neighbor's, is a welcome addition to Ainu society. Ainu folklore abundantly reflects this concern with the preservation and increase of the human population. Thus the most dreadful demons are the ones which exterminate Ainu settlements, and the role of not only slaying the demons but also replenishing the depopulated settlements is assigned to the Ainu culture hero (see "Demons," Chapter 6). The Ainu desire for many children and for increased population in general is an important factor explaining many of their beliefs and customs, especially those related to birth, marriage, and kinship.

For example, the birth of twins, especially when both are males, is the most important and most welcome type of birth. A twin birth is called, literally, a "gift from the deities," and the twins require special treatment. When they sleep they must be placed on the most sacred side of the house, and their belongings, such as clothes, may never be placed on the rear (west) side of the house. A girl who is born into a family immediately after male twins is called a "servant of the deities" and is also treated by the family with special care. Husko was one of these, although one of her twin brothers died shortly after birth. Considering herself to enjoy a favored relationship with the deities, she made a special effort to learn the Ainu way of life. The twin who comes out of the mother first is considered the younger of the pair, representing a reversal of the American practice. Twins are rare among the Ainu, and other multiple births, being practically nonexistent, do not receive any particular recognition.

INFANCY

At birth a child is regarded as affiliated with both of its parents. Although the responsibility of feeding and caring for a newborn baby rests primarily with the mother, the infant is constantly held, not only by its family members and relatives but also by other adult women and children of the settlement. Ainu mothers, who show little possessiveness toward their young offspring, are generally not concerned about their babies becoming spoiled or about possible differences of opinion with other adults over child-rearing techniques and philosophies. An infant often spends most of its waking hours strapped on someone's back by a belt which goes around the carrier's forehead and the infant's body.

Besides the belt, there are two other types of carriers which are used until the infant reaches two years of age. One, called *čahka*, is made from a hollowed-out tree trunk. Hare or puppy fur is placed in it and the infant is positioned so that its legs may hang out. The carrier is hung from the ceiling with a rope, thereby protecting the infant from fleas and mice, both of which are abundant in Ainu houses. When the baby cries someone swings it. During the summer diapers are not used. Instead, a hole is made in the carrier so that when the infant relieves itself, the waste falls to the ground. During the cold season no hole is made. The infant then wears a hare or puppy fur diaper into which the aforementioned soft substance made from the rotten parts of a tree trunk is inserted. Its soft and absorbent texture is comfortable for the baby. Only the tree substance, not the fur, must be changed as it becomes soiled. Another carrier, called *amčahka*, is made from birchbark and is used at night and during the daytime when the mother carries the infant in her arms.

Although many others may participate in the care of the infant during the daytime, at night it lies right next to the mother in a birchbark carrier. The warmth of the mother's body is believed to keep the baby healthy. This sleeping arrangement often continues until a younger baby displaces an old one. It is not uncommon for a child to sleep beside either mother or father until the teens. There seems to be no pattern as to the sex of the child and the parent beside whom it sleeps. The

Ainu description of sleeping arrangements thus displays an interesting discrepancy between what the Ainu say they do and what they actually do. As we saw earlier, there is a definite hierarchy among the four sides of the Ainu house, and in theory the rules as to who sits and sleeps where are well defined. Yet in actuality, the rigidity of the rules yields to the fact of human interactions.

One day while Husko was describing Ainu sleeping arrangements, her granddaughter dropped in with her newborn baby. Husko turned to her and said, "What's wrong with young mothers these days? She lets a baby sleep alone and goes to her husband's side." Husko's comment about her granddaughter reminded me of my own surprise on seeing a shocked expression on my (American) husband's face when I placed my oldest son in our bed on the night we returned from the hospital. During my days in Japan, a newborn baby always slept next to his mother, and I could not place him alone in a crib. Shortly after Husko made the comment about her granddaughter, she pointed to her cousin, a man of about 60 years of age, who was visiting us as usual, and explained that he slept beside his father until he was married. This comment sounded strange to me, since in the segment of Japanese society in which I was raised a girl may continue to go to her mother's or even father's side at night, but a boy may not. These comments by Husko make me realize how each culture exercises a profound influence on the psychology of the individual at the level of unconscious patterning as well as of conscious thought processes.

The period of nursing may last as long as two or three years. Sometimes when a younger sibling is born before the older one is weaned, the mother nurses both of them. The Ainu have a special leek gruel for women with insufficient milk. They say that this dish is so effective that it can enable almost any woman to nurse. If a mother dies or falls ill, some other woman with milk will nurse the infant in addition to her own. If the baby is a motherless female, this woman often acquires the baby permanently, but if a motherless male, the father generally takes him back after the nursing period is over. Usually, however, male children are not strongly preferred to female. Partly because women nurse children for a prolonged period of time the Ainu do not make special dishes for babies. The mother simply chews regular food, especially good fish like salmon, before she gives it to her child. Serving both as food and teether, a sparerib of a bear, a hare, or a dog is often given to a baby. Later this is replaced by a hunk of meat skewed by a stick. A child can hold the sparerib or stick and chew the meat at his own pace.

One of the most serious concerns about infants is sickness, much of which is believed to be caused by evil spirits. The Ainu take various kinds of precautions, which are directed toward the exorcism of evil spirits. *Pon tennehpo*, the term for "infant," itself embodies this concern. Meaning "a small wet (with urine) child," the term is used to discourage the approach of demons. An infant may also be wrapped in rags, since evil spirits do not like dirty rags. Similarly, a baby's clothing may be made from a belt or garment worn by an adult of either sex over the genitals, as these clothes are believed capable of forcing away evil spirits. It is also believed that demons frequently will substitute an ailing infant of their own for a healthy human baby if they can kidnap a child while its mother is out of the house (this explanation is advanced for some types of deformities). Therefore, when an infant is left alone, weapons such as knives are arranged beside it so that they may come alive and attack any demons sneaking about the child.

An Ainu child does not necessarily receive a name at birth, and there is no set date for naming a child. Often a person is addressed and referred to by such terms as "child" or "youngster" and kinship terms such as "younger sister" and "uncle" even when there are no kinship ties between the two individuals (see Chapter 5). Yet at some point during his lifetime he receives a common name, and often also a holy name. Not all the Ainu have a holy name, which has to be "revealed" during a shamanistic rite. Some are named after a deity, but the meanings of holy names are often unclear. A common name is often colorful in meaning and has to do with something specifically about the individual. Thus some time after Husko's younger sister was born, the family started to call the older daughter "Husko," which means "old," and the younger one "Asiri," which means "new." The aforementioned precautions against illnesses caused by evil spirits and demons often affect the choice of a name. One man who was a good singer-narrator of epic poems was called "Čohčonke," the belt covering the male genitals. Another man's name was Osomaruype ("bowel-mover"). He used to dirty his pants when small and, for his own protection, the evil spirits were informed of this. Other names reflect experiences of later life, as in the case of a lady's man who was named "Čikoro Henke" (elder who has a penis), or an elderly woman named Nuwah Ahči, who because of her weak heart breathed heavily (nuwah). However, the Ainu do not seem to associate the literal meanings of these names with the individuals bearing them, just as we do not always associate "Mr. Carpenter" with carpentry. Thus a famous shaman or a revered elder may have a "funny" name which in no way interferes with his dignity or the respect granted him by his fellow Ainu. Only when the Ainu are reminded of how these names originated, or when they are asked to explain the meaning of a "funny" name, do they chuckle in amusement. Even more fundamental in understanding Ainu names are the facts that most of these names are given because of the belief in evil spirits and that the Ainu regard sex and related parts of the body more matter of factly and openly than many other peoples. Furthermore, the Ainu naming practice reveals that, despite their general emphasis on family and kinship ties, they do not have family names, and an individual's kinship identity is in no way expressed in his name. An Ainu name expresses something about the experiences or personality of the individual.

CHILDHOOD

The children beyond the stage of infancy are collectively called hekači. Younger ones may be specified as pon hekači (small youngsters), older ones as poro hekači (big youngsters), males as iwanehpo, and females as merekopo. The transition from the infant stage to that of youngster, or hekači, is gradual, without accompanying rituals. It is a significant transition, however, since the child is no longer indulged by adults, but must start sharing the responsibilities of life. Thus when fishing boats return, everyone in the community except infants, pregnant women, the sick, and the extremely old goes to the shore to unload and dry the fish. Children are expected to assist not only in this but also in plant gathering and various other adult activities. Girls carry their younger siblings on their backs and fetch water for cooking and other purposes from the sea or river. They start early to learn to cook, sew, and embroider. Boys help their fathers obtain firewood and starters such as birchbark and twigs. Even in games and play children simulate adult activities. For example, boys target practice with miniature bows and arrows, spears, or other hunting weapons, aiming at a bear or seal made of pieces of wood, twigs, and grass. They play another game in which they roll a circular wooden ring and compete in striking its center with a stick, simulating spearing or harpooning.

YOUNG ADULTHOOD

Growing Up To Be a Young Man   Biological changes are only one aspect of the gradual transition from a boy to a young man. The biological changes in a male are collectively expressed as "when the pubic region darkens (with hair)," and at some point a boy is given a covering for his genitals. More important, however, is his performance in male roles. Thus when a boy successfully shoots down a bird, his boyhood hair style is changed to that of a man. Although the front hair of both boys and men is shaved off, in the case of boys a small portion in the center is left and a small triangular piece of material with beads attached to it, called *hohčiri*, is hung from it with a string. This hair style is said to have been taught to the Ainu by a sea god (killer whale) who married an Ainu woman from *Yohohkinay*, near the former Russo-Japanese border. A year after she was married to the deity, she came back to show her baby, who wore this hair style, to her parents (see the details of the story in Chapter 6). As a boy proves his hunting skill, the *hohčiri* is removed and the front hair is shaved off. The requirement of shooting down a bird, however, became lax in the recent past, and boys simply changed their hair style some time during the mid-teens. The most significant event for a boy during the period of this study is the time when he is given two knives. One is used exclusively for carving the *inaw* ritual sticks and the other for other purposes. As we saw earlier, carpentry is one of the most important skills of adult males and it has religious significance. During the period of the gradual transition to manhood, a boy goes through the exciting experiences of his first hunting and fishing and participates in adult male activities progressively more as he grows older.

Growing Up To Be a Young Woman   Biological changes affect females more than they do males. The most important of these changes is menstruation. Menstruation is understood as a process during which old blood in a woman's body is discharged while water she drinks turns into new blood, causing women to be thirsty during their menstrual periods. Accompanying pains and cramps are considered to be caused by the old blood which "walks around" in the body before its exit. No direct relationship between menstruation and the reproductive process is assumed. With her first menstruation, a girl is given a protective covering made with hare hide and padded with dried grass to absorb the discharge. Although her biological change does not involve a ritual, she must at this time assume a completely new set of behavioral patterns, stemming from the blood taboo, discussed earlier. Thus her clothes may not be hung where there is even the slightest possibility of a man passing under them; a man will be contaminated by the lingering smell even when the clothes are not stained. She may not go fishing on the lake during her menstrual period; lake fishing is otherwise permissible for women. She may not even participate in the bear ceremony until her menstrual period is over. When it is over, she must perform a purification rite by waving a spruce branch and artimisia grass (wormwood) around her body; only then can she join the celebration. If and when she becomes a shaman, she may not perform a rite during her menstrual period. The increase in the size of the breasts also requires modification in behavior. From the onset of this sign of puberty, women must be extremely modest and keep the breasts covered at all times. Although the behavioral

Little girls carrying their sibling and loads. (Courtesy of C. Chard)

change resulting from breast enlargement is not as extensive as that caused by menstruation, the expression of "buttoning up all the way" (to cover the breasts) is frequently used, especially in oral literature, to symbolically denote the maturity of a woman.

Tattoo, an important symbol of adult women, may be first applied as early as the mid-teens, but its application has no formalized correlation with puberty, marriage, or any other stage of a woman's life cycle. The tattoo is dark blue in color and is applied to the face in the following order: above the upper lip in the center; below the lower lip in the center; the rest of the area above the upper lip; and the rest of the area below the lower lip. The technique of tattooing, according to a myth (Tale 15 in Ohnuki-Tierney 1969b), was taught by *tukusis* trout who turned themselves into Ainu women and transmitted the women's skills of weaving, dyeing, and tattooing. The body of this type of *Salvelinus* trout has bluish spots resembling the tattoo marks. The tattoo is applied by making fine incisions in parallel lines with a knife and rubbing a mixture of herring oil and soot from the bottom of a pan. The soot is specially made by burning birchbark. Perhaps the womanhood symbolism of tattooing is related to the use of soot, which is believed to be made by the most important female deity of the Ainu, Grandmother Hearth. The application of the tattoo is an extremely painful procedure, sometimes resulting in swelling of the mouth, rendering a person unable to eat. However, the tattoo is a symbol of female beauty and, often, status. Thus only wives of men of higher social standing may apply tattooing all around the mouth: many have it only in the center above and below the lips.

Tattooing, however, is not a well-developed practice among the Ainu of the northwest coast. No woman among them was able to apply a tattoo, and women desiring beautification had to wait until a woman with the skill came to visit from the east coast. This woman came only to larger settlements such as *Rayčiska* and *Ustomonaypo*. Hence some women farther north had never had a chance to be tattooed, whereas others were able to be tattooed while visiting one of these settlements when the tattoo specialist was present. Both the tattooing method and the cultural values ascribed to the custom, that is, its beauty and use as a status symbol, are well entrenched among the Ainu of the northwest coast. Perhaps indicating its southern origin, tattooing is elaborately developed among the Hokkaido Ainu women, who have it around the mouth, extending over the cheeks to the ears, as well as on the hands and arms and in one locality between the eye and the eyebrow. Among the Hokkaido Ainu, the custom of tattooing is said to have been transmitted by the aforementioned small-statured ancestors (Ainu Bunka Hozon Taisaku Kyogikai 1970:131–135).

A child gradually becomes a young adult, and none of the events described above serves by itself as a rite of passage. The young adults are collectively called *sukuh utah*—if male *sukuh ohkayo*, if female *sukuh mahtekuh*. One of the most significant experiences for a young adult is marriage. When asked, the Ainu state that premarital relations are frowned upon. However, they proceed to explain that should a girl's suitor creep into her bed at night, she is not supposed to create a commotion. If the girl's protest makes the visit known to others, especially the neighbors, her parents may have to pay a fine to the young man for his loss of face through their daughter's careless conduct. In the main the Ainu are tolerant of premarital relations and illegitimate children.

Marriage Marriange is often arranged by the parents or other kinsmen of a child, either at its birth or more frequently between the ages of three and five. At the time of engagement, the uppermost button of a boy's garment, called *nohpokun numah*, is given to the fiancée, who uses it as the uppermost button on her garment. From this time she is formally engaged to the boy. Such an engagement may be broken later, however, should one party fall in love with and wish to marry someone else. The Ainu way of proposal is efficient and nonverbal. When a man wishes to propose, he passes a dish of food, which he has already partially consumed, to the woman of his choice. If she wishes to accept his proposal, she will finish the food. The average age of marriage for a girl is somewhere in the mid-teens, while that of a man falls in his early to mid-twenties. The time of the wedding is fixed only in terms of the month, but not the day, which has no numerical specification as ours does. Usually the groom's family sends a messenger to the bride's family, if it resides at a separate settlement, to notify its members of the month. Some time before the wedding, the groom comes to reside with the bride's family and starts to help her parents in their daily activities—a custom called "bride service" by anthropologists. The Ainu's own explanation of this practice is that, since they do not have money as do the Japanese, the groom pays for his bride with his own labor. One of the advantages of this custom of beginning the bride service prior to actual marriage, according to the Ainu, is that this period gives the groom a chance to back out of the arrangement. He can simply leave the bride's house and marriage is considered not to have taken place. There is no such option for the bride. This piece of information is another example illustrating how cultural norms are modified in actual practice to accommodate individual differences. Thus the Ainu state that a marriage should be arranged by the parents, and yet not only do individuals often marry on the basis of romantic feelings, but a young man can successfully reject an arrangement made by his parents.

Dowry is given by the bride's father to the groom only in the rare event that the bride's father is a chief or some other extremely wealthy man. A dowry consists of such Ainu treasures as libation-prayer sticks, Japanese lacquerware, and swords. Like some anthropologists, the Ainu explain that a bride with dowry will be treated better by her husband. Examples show, however, that dowry does not necessarily guarantee better treatment, although it does demonstrate the wealth and social status of the bride's faher.

Marriage, like all other ceremonies, must take place some time between the new moon and the full moon. No wedding can take place when people are very busy, especially with fishing. The ceremony is brief and simple, involving only the members of the bride's family, and sometimes those of the groom's family. For several days after the wedding, the groom continues to help the bride's parents. Then the newlyweds go to the settlement of the groom's father. Only when the groom is the oldest son does the couple live in the house of his parents. In other cases, they set up a separate household in the same settlement. There are no culturally prescribed or proscribed rules of behavior toward one's affines. An average individual seems to marry more than once, not infrequently several times, and divorce takes place without formality and without involving a third party in the matter.

Procreation The most important factor in any marriage is the producing of offspring. The mechanism of conception is understood in the following manner. Every woman has a tube in the lower part of her body, but this tube is open only at a certain time of the month. For most women, this time is believed to be during the two successive moons or just as a new moon is coming out. If a woman has intercourse during this period, the man's semen, which is considered as blood, mixes with the woman's blood to produce an egg, as in the case of fish. Every woman has a limited supply of eggs, and when the supply runs out she can no longer bear children. When a man's blood (semen) is weak, then he is "sterile."

Positive measures are taken when a couple cannot seem to produce as many natural children as they would like. A woman may make a charm from the dried ovary of such animals as a harbor seal, a bear, or a dog. She then wraps it in a piece of material and fastens it around her waist like a belt. There is no counterpart of this method for a man, who, however, has two alternatives. First, he may take another wife. Second, a childless man, having failed to father children with two or more women, is culturally sanctioned to arrange for his wife's impregnation by one of his brothers or friends. Husko's father's half-brother (son of the same father by a different mother), who headed the most prominent family at the *Rayčiska* settlement and thus was eager to have an heir, asked his half-brother (Husko's father's full brother) to produce offspring with his co-wife, and the result was successful. This method, however, is not frequently used.

Although these methods are available, adoption is the most frequent resource for a childless couple, who treat an adopted child just as they would a natural child. Only in terms of marriage regulations are the actual blood lines of the child traced. There is no fixed age of adoption. No special ceremony is performed at the time of adoption, although occasionally the adoptive parents offer a gift, such as a box of dried fish, to the biological parents.

In addition to this voluntary adoption, there is another type of adoption prescribed by tradition. That is, a child born on the day when another child among its relatives dies must be given away to the parents of the dead child. The parents have no say in the matter. Thus when Husko's newborn baby died, she and her husband were ready to adopt a child born of their relatives on the same day. They planned to take into the family both the infant and its mother, who was blind. The infant died a few days after its birth, and thus the adoption never took place.

These positive measures taken to ensure that a couple has children indicate that the Ainu, while claiming that children are an expression of the deities' favor toward the couple, do not consider actual casses of barrenness as proof of the deities' disfavor.

There are various taboos for women during pregnancy. The most important one is that a woman may not go to the shore. If she does, the fish will melt away, since the fish-producing sea deity dislikes the smell of the blood at the time of approaching childbirth. Other taboo regulations are minor behavioral rules; for example, a pregnant woman must not twine threads, since this may cause her intestines to twist. A dehydrated bear intestine is considered most effective in inducing an easy labor, and a pregnant woman places one in a piece of material and wraps it around her waist. One of the most touching human experiences I had during my fieldwork was when Husko gave me a bear intestine which she had been saving for a long time to give to her daughter or granddaughter. Since I was in the last stage of pregnancy as I was leaving the field, she gave it to me as a farewell gift and performed a shamanistic rite, praying to her deities to protect me during my trip back to the United States and during subsequent childbirth.

An expectant father must also observe some taboo regulations. For example, he must not drive nails all the way into wood while engaging in carpentry, since if his wife goes into a hard labor, he must be able to pull the nails out quickly. Intercourse, taboo during a woman's menstrual period as well as after childbirth, is considered a welcome gesture to the fetus on the part of the father during the last stage of pregnancy.

For her childbirth, a parturient woman usually goes to her mother's home, even when it is located in a separate settlement. There is no culturally defined group of kinswomen to provide assistance; her mother and any other women available offer their help. In small settlements on the northwest coast there may not be many people to help, especially if plant gathering has drawn the women away from the settlement. Thus every woman must be prepared to give birth by herself. Until the child's umbilical cord drops off, the mother is considered especially contagious, and men who come in contact with her must refrain from hunting and fishing. Therefore, when childbirth approaches, the woman's family must prepare a special hut, called *po:koro čise* (child-bearing house), where she can seclude herself. If there is an empty house nearby, the pregnant woman is moved there. Otherwise, in the summer, a tepee-shaped grass hut is constructed next to the family's house. In winter, weather disallows this arrangement, and the women take over the family house and the menfolk must meanwhile stay with relatives and neighbors. Under any of these circumstances a man can talk with the parturient woman from outside, but may never enter the place of her confinement.

An important rule surrounding childbirth is that the placenta must be wrapped in a grass mat, brought over to a wooded area, and placed in the crotch of a bifurcated branch. An interesting sidelight regarding this custom is that Ainu stories from various parts of Sakhalin unanimously relate that a feud with the neighboring Oroks started when the latter ate an Ainu placenta, mistaking it as some animal's intestines. This, as noted earlier, illustrates to what extent the Ainu single out the raw-food consumption of the Oroks for criticism.

When the child's umbilical cord drops off, the mother and child return to their usual dwelling and a simple purification rite is performed. Only then may men approach the mother without fear of contamination. While there are no food regulations for pregnant women, postpartum behavioral rules center around food. There are special dishes to be eaten, while several kinds of fish, meat, and plant foods are taboo. Intercourse is taboo until bleeding ceases.

Young Adulthood—A Preparatory Stage The young adults are important members of Ainu society, playing the central role in economic activities. However, just as the stage of youth is preparatory for that of adulthood, young adulthood is preliminary to that of the aged. Thus young adults must gradually learn the aforementioned (Chapter 3) language of the aged. If male, they must also learn the language of the deities, as well as the rules and regulations governing Ainu rituals. Equally important is the knowledge of Ainu social behavior, prescribed on the basis of the individual's sex and age, which are the two most important determinants of Ainu social status. Thus if a woman sees a man coming toward her on the same path from the other direction, she must make a wide curve toward the side of the path in order not to approach the man too closely. If the man is an elder, she must step toward the side and wait until he passes by. The visiting etiquette between two individuals who have not seen each other for a while is even more elaborate and ritualized. Coughing several times in front of the host's house as an announcement of one's arrival and, for men, the reciprocal filling of tobacco pipes are only minor features of this intricate system. Most elaborate of all are the greetings between two elders when the host has lost two family or kin members within a short period, or has no relatives. Although an occasion for such greetings arises only infrequently, these salutations resemble theatrical performances in their oratory and expression of emotions. They duly impress observers as an illustration of the grace and sagacity of the elders.

THE AGED

The aged are the most revered members of Ainu society and are political leaders as well as guardians of religion, oral literature, and other important traditions, inclusively termed *aynu pu:ri* (human [Ainu] way, manners). Through the use of the language of the aged and that of the deities, male elders in particular enjoy their exclusive claim over two important realms in Ainu life, both of which involve abundant use of these two types of diction. Thus male elders alone can dedicate formulaic prayers during religious ceremonies as well as recite the *hawki* tales of the most sacred genre of Ainu oral tradition, as we saw in Chapter 3. External symbols, such as the aforementioned white garment made exclusively of nettle fiber with red embroidery, conspicuously support their privileged status in the society. Even the aged females acquire certain privileges that are forbidden to younger women, who occupy the lowest position in the society. Thus they may in special instances participate in such otherwise male territory as the law (see Chapter 5), and the person who takes the major responsibility in raising a bear cub, the supreme deity, must be an aged female. The privileged status of the aged is based on the belief that they are closest to the deities and hence the most sacred members of Ainu society. Therefore, just as the Ainu may not pronounce the names of their deities out loud, they may not use the names of revered elders. Hence, they resort to teknonymy, addressing and referring to an elder as so-and-so's grandfather or grandmother.

The above information suggests that the Ainu, who do not count their age as we do, set up these stages of one's life with an emphasis on the individual's performance of behavioral roles. Thus, a particular elder is in the aged (*onneru*) category not so much because he has passed a certain chronological point in his life, say 50 years, but because he is capable of handling religious and political matters and because old age in the Ainu view is a block of time in human life when humans are closest to the deities in their status.

DEATH—THE END OF HUMAN LIFE IN THIS WORLD

The end of human life in this world, of course, is death, which to the Ainu also marks a rebirth of the deceased in the world of the dead. Although death can occur at any point in the life cycle, for the sake of convenience, beliefs and rituals concerning death are discussed here in the last section of this chapter.

The Ainu conceive of the phenomenon of death as being caused by a permanent departure of the person's soul from the body, although the description of mortuary and burial procedure seems to indicate that the separation and fusion of the soul and the body are ambiguous throughout this period. The soul lingers beside the empty body during the funeral. If and when a proper funeral is given, it travels to the world of the dead Ainu, where it re-enters the body, which somehow is also transferred there. The soul sometimes is said to travel in the form of a bird. Unless a proper funeral is given, however, the soul is unable to make this trip and rest in peace. Hence it listlessly lingers in the world of the living Ainu, troubling its survivors in order to remind them to perform a proper funeral. All funerals must take place after the sun passes the meridian, and usually are performed toward evening.

The Ainu explicitly classify deaths into several categories. The place of death is the determinant in this classification, and each category requires a different type of funeral. The major division of deaths is between those having taken place inside the house versus those having taken place outside, with the latter category being further subdivided. Deaths which take place inside the house are ordinary deaths, and these call forth two types of funeral: those for ordinary Ainu and those for chiefs and other prominent men.

Funerals—Deaths Inside a House   When an ordinary Ainu dies inside the house, the women start making as a shroud an ordinary garment but without embroidery. For the ritual feasting for the dead, they prepare dishes which are also ordinary, although often the favorites of the deceased are included. When the ground is not frozen, the men dig a hole in the community cemetery located in the hilly area behind the settlement. The men also must make parts for the coffin, to be constructed at the burial ground after the deceased is brought there. Characteristically, the coffin is made of Sakhalin fir—a tree associated with deaths and sickness. Some men must also gather and lay at the doorway certain charms against evil spirits and demons. There are stems of a plant related to sweetbrier (*otaruh ni:* in Ainu), leaves of a plant in the carrot family (*siwkina kutu* in Ainu), leaves of a plant related to cow parsnip (*situri kina kutu* in Ainu), a piece of fishnet, and two small stones. The plants are believed to expel the evil spirits and demons which are particularly prone to capture the souls of the deceased and prevent their safe journey to the world of the dead Ainu. The stones and fishnet are placed not only at the doorway but also later in the coffin, regardless of the sex of the deceased; the deceased can put up the fishnet with stone sinkers and thus prevent evil spirits and demons from coming close to him. The Ainu choose a piece of fishnet with a small mesh, since it will turn into a net with large mesh in the world of the dead Ainu; there many things become exact opposite to what they are in the world of the living Ainu. Thus the deceased is clad in a shroud with the left flap in front overlapping the right, although a living person wears his garment with the right flap overlapping the left. Upon arrival at the world of the dead Ainu, he will be suitably dressed, since things get reversed there.

After a ritual meal for the deceased in the presence of all the relatives who have gathered by this time, often a few days after the death has taken place, the deceased is carried legs first out of the house wrapped in a grass mat. This posture is considered to guarantee that he will not look back into his beloved house and decide to stay there. At the burial ground, the coffin is constructed and the corpse is placed in an extended position, at which time only half of the grass mat is used to wrap the dead. The mat is cut at several places, so that the soul can get out of the body. Also, if a person dies of any stomach trouble, a small cut must be made on the stomach with a knife, and a piece of material used as a bandage; otherwise the survivors would also suffer from similar stomach illnesses. This procedure is unpleasant for the survivors, as it was for Husko when one of her daughters died with a swollen stomach.

Burial goods are placed in the coffin. If the deceased is a male, these may include a pipe and eating utensils or, if a female, kitchen utensils. After the coffin is closed a small dirt mound is raised over it. Then the remaining half of the grass mat is cut into pieces and spread over the mound. The tomb marker is a trunk of Sakhalin fir from which the upper half of the bark is peeled. This process, however, is possible only during the warm season. When the ground is frozen, as it is for more than half the year, the Ainu simply place two logs on the ground and place the sealed coffin on top of them. In explaining the cold-season burial process, the Ainu emphasize that their custom is quite different from that of the Oroks, who make a special raised structure and then place the coffin upon it.

No less important than the funeral and its preparation is the purification rite performed at the house of the deceased while the mourners are at the cemetery. This rite is performed by an elderly woman or man familiar with the ceremonial details. It involves the removal of dust and soot from the house with a fir branch made into a ritual stick. Particular attention is paid to the ritual cleaning of the hearth and related objects. The purpose is to eliminate the contamination caused by the death and to light a new and clean fire, thereby ensuring the rebirth of the Grandmother Hearth. Thus the ashes in the hearth are removed and new sand from the shore replaces the old. The soot formed by the old fire at the bottom of the pans is meticulously removed. Furthermore, all the firewood gathered before the death took place, which is therefore contaminated, must be thrown away and freshly chopped wood brought in. Likewise the old pair of ritual sticks which had been offered to the Grandmother Hearth must be removed. When the mourners return from the cemetery, they must wash their hands with water and eat a special dish with minced leek, which has been cooked in the freshly cleaned hearth.

A few days after the funeral, another ash-renewal rite is performed and a new pair of ritual sticks for the Grandmother Hearth is made. Only then does this elaborate funerary procedure come to an end.

A Funeral for a Chief   The death of a chief or other great man requires a special and altogether different type of mortuary treatment. There are four main points of difference from the procedure outlined above: an incision into the body; the building of a special rooflike structure on the coffin; the placing of the coffin on two logs on the ground regardless of the season; and a special location for the coffin in the cemetery. During the period of our study there were two men whom the Ainu honored with this type of funeral. In both cases Husko's father, who was the only one with a detailed knowledge of the custom, provided the instructions. Those involved did not, however, cut open the dead, although they knew of this having been done in the recent past. One of the favorite Ainu folktales (Tale 23 of Ohnuki-Tierney 1969b) also describes this custom. In this story, upon the death of two brothers who were the great leaders of the Ainu during a war against the Oroks, the brothers' hearts were opened by their people. A bundle of hair was found in the heart of one, and the other's heart was made of white flint. This explained to the Ainu why they were so great. The elaborate funerary procedure for deceased chiefs by the Sakhalin Ainu caught the observant eyes of early Japanese explorers, and we fortunately have some descriptions of the custom dating from the very beginning of the nineteenth century (Kondo 1804:n.p.; Mamiya 1855:340). Both descriptions indicate that the Ainu of that time took out all the intestines of a deceased chief and kept the body for a prolonged period of time, while daily washing and drying the emptied stomach, thus preventing its decay. Mamiya's account further tells that the entire process was the responsibility of the deceased chief's wife. If the body started to rot, she was killed and her funeral preceded that of her husband. We therefore see that up to the ethnographic present it remained customary to give a chief a special funeral, although the incision of the body and accompanying features had been foregone.

The World of the Dead Ainu   All Ainu, regardless of social status, who die inside the house are believed to resume their life in the world of the dead Ainu. The Ainu term *yayasirika* (reborn) is somewhat misleading for those who are familiar with the idea of reincarnation. The Ainu concept of rebirth does not necessarily involve rebirth as an infant. Thus, when the Ainu say that the dead person is reborn in the world of the dead Ainu, he is believed to resume his life at whichever point he left it at the time of death; he does so, however, in the world of the dead.

All that which is known about the world of the dead Ainu comes from those who died a "temporary death." I have not been able to precisely identify these temporary deaths in terms of our own experience. They refer to a person sleeping an unusually long time or losing consciousness for a prolonged period. At any rate, during these temporary deaths, which seem to happen quite commonly (Husko experienced two during her lifetime), the soul of a person leaves his body and briefly visits the world of the dead. There are certain themes which are emphasized by all who have "died" a temporary death and later relate their experiences. The stories always start with the narrator walking or crawling through a pitch-dark and narrow tunnel or cave which connects the two worlds. He then almost always emerges behind the settlement of his dead relatives. Listening to these stories, one receives the picture of a tunnel under a mountain connecting back to back the two worlds, each the mirror image of the other. In fact, the Ainu term for the world of the dead is "*auru un kotan*," meaning an adjacent settlement. In or near many of the Ainu settlements there is actually a cave which the Ainu designate as the one connecting the two worlds. The locations of these caves or tunnels, however, vary from seashore to hillside.

For the most part the world of the living Ainu is a blueprint for the world of the dead. Just like the summer settlements of the living Ainu, the settlements of the dead are located near the shore, and the dead engage in the familiar activities of fishing, hunting, plant gathering, weaving, and so on. Dogs, the faithful companions of the Ainu in life, are there, as well as demons and evil spirits. Despite these similarities between the two worlds, however, certain things, such as the seasons of the year, are always exactly opposite. Thus an Ainu who visits there when it is winter in this world finds his deceased relatives engaged in catching and drying fish. Although a living Ainu can visit the world of the dead, communication between the living and the dead does not or must not take place. Neither can the dead see the living visitor, nor hear his voice. Thus every visitor relates that his deceased parents, uncles, and aunts, for example, passed in front of him without noticing his presence. The dead would often wonder why their dogs were barking; the dogs alone seem to notice the visitor's presence because of the smell of the living.

There is yet another piece of information about the world of the dead which concerns the punishment of the wicked, such as murderers, thieves, liars, and wife stealers. This information, however, is offered only when the Ainu are questioned as to where "bad" Ainu go after their deaths. Then they explain that the most severe offenders of the Ainu laws are to be boiled in hot water in a huge iron caldron, while minor offenders are punished, purified, and then allowed to join their deceased kinsmen. The punishment of the wicked takes place somewhere right in the world of the dead Ainu. The description of the manner of punishment, such as the use of caldrons, suggests that this part of the information may very well have been added to the traditional view after the Ainu had been exposed to the Japanese Buddhist concept of hell.

The Ainu in other parts of Sakhalin and Hokkaido seem to have similar notions about the world of the dead. They share such themes as the parallels of life-style between the two worlds, the reversal of some temporal units between the two worlds, and the concepts of a cave or a tunnel serving as a passage between the two spheres. However, there are some significant differences. For example, according to reports, the Hokkaido Ainu emphasize "hell" and often describe the world of the dead as located underground. Some of them believe that there are two worlds of the dead: one for the ordinary Ainu and the other, located farther below, for the wicked (for detailed references to the Hokkaido Ainu notions of the world after death, see Ohnuki-Tierney 1968:156–158). Trying to understand the Ainu notions of death and life after death is indeed a challenging task, precisely because we have both in Christian and Buddhist traditions their versions of such concepts as rebirth, lift after death, hell, and underworld, which are quasi-equivalent to the Ainu concepts. It is all to easy for an outside investigator to translate the Ainu term into equivalent words of his own language, and at the same time to erroneously translate Ainu notions into pseudo-equivalent concepts of the Christian or Buddhist world view. The world of the dead Ainu as conceived by the northwest coast Ainu is a world just like that of the living Ainu, and it should not be perceived within any framework which includes "hell" and "heaven" as integral parts of the world after death.

Funerals—Deaths Outside a House In contrast to those who die in the confines of the house and hence go to the regular world of the dead, deaths taking place outside require altogether different types of funerals. In all these cases the corpse is neither taken back to the house nor buried in the regular part of the cemetery. Furthermore, the souls of these dead may travel elsewhere than to the world of the dead Ainu. The "outside deaths," or *soyo isam*, of the Ainu include deaths in water; deaths caused by bears; deaths of senile and insane people who have been intentionally placed in a grass hut near the house; and all other types of deaths taking place outside, including suicides and deaths caused by sudden and lethal illnesses. Only the first two types of deaths will be dealt with here. Of all deaths taking place outside the home, the deaths in water are most dreaded by the Ainu and call for elaborate funerals. Although the Ainu term for this type of death is *atuy isam* (sea death), it includes all deaths in rivers, lakes, and the sea, with causes ranging from drowning to supposed strangulation by a giant octopus. The deceased's family members and relatives first build a tepee-shaped hut made of grass mats on the sandy beach at the spot where the deceased was last seen. Then they build a bonfire which must be kept burning until the corpse gets washed ashore; the bonfire is believed to attract the corpse. A messenger is dispatched to all the related settlements to gather relatives for the funeral. While the men make parts for the coffin, the women prepare a funeral meal and sew a shroud All of these activities must take place at the hut. If found, the body must be buried in the grass field next to the sandy beach and not in the cemetery. In the absence of the corpse, the same ritual must be carried out with an empty coffin. The funeral procession from the hut to the burial ground consists of male elders and older women who follow the elders' lead. They perform an exorcism rite during the procession, males swinging their swords right and left, while shouting at every swing of the sword, and females doing the same with their knives. The swings of the swords and knives are believed to kill evil spirits which try to snatch the soul of the deceased. Instead of a regular grave post, a small altar made of ritual sticks and called *inausi* is built at the place of burial. Then the house where the deceased formerly lived must be torn down with axes, no matter how recently it may have been built, and the lumber may not be reused. The soul of a person who has died in water is believed to go to the world of the deities up in the sky. During Husko's lifetime, she observed this particular kind of funeral rite three times.

Regardless of actual location of happening, be it on the beach or on a mountain, deaths caused by bears are called *kimo isam* (mountain death), since bears are mountain deities. Ainu killed by bears are believed to visit the world of the mountain deities before they go to the world of the dead Ainu. Hence, a special kind of mortuary and burial treatment is required. The funeral has to be given immediately and at the exact place where the bear killed the deceased. The victim must also be buried at the spot. No coffin is used. If other men succeed in killing the guilty bear, after making an incision in its stomach to permit the soul's escape, they insert a piece of wood in its mouth as a punishment for biting and killing a man. It is believed that the wood will prevent the bear from eating in the world of dead bears. The Ainu then dig a fairly deep hole and place the bear at the bottom and the victim on top of it. This manner of burial parallels the burial of a human murderer, who also is placed at the bottom of a hole under his victim (Chapter 5). Thus the manner of burial seems to symbolically identify the bear as a murderer. After dirt is placed over the hole, an altar made of ritual sticks is built at the spot. Only males and older women are allowed to participate in the funeral of a bear's victim. Unlike deaths in water, however, neither exorcism nor the destruction of the house of the victim is required.

Features common to the funerals of those dying in water and those killed by bears are the erection of an altar at the burial site and the belief that the souls involved go to the worlds of deities—to the sky in the first case and to the mountains in the second. It seems then that the Ainu deify, at least temporarily, people who die of deaths in these two categories. The survivors regularly visit their altars, at least three times a year, and renew the ritual sticks. Also, whenever someone passes by an altar of this kind or spots it on land while passing in a boat, he must perform an informal rite, offering tobacco, leek, and other possessions at hand which are suitable for offerings.

The Ainu have an elaborate complex in regard to death, the last stage of one's life in this world. The purpose of meticulous treatment is to ensure that the soul of the dead goes to its proper place and continues to live. The dead are an integral part of the lives of the living Ainu; the deceased ancestors protect the Ainu, but if not treated properly, they can cause troubles. The importance which the Ainu place on the proper treatment of the dead must be understood in this context of close interaction between the living Ainu and their deceased ancestors. Therefore, although we frequently encounter statements emphasizing the Ainu fear of the deceased, it seems that the Ainu are not so much afraid of the dead as they are afraid of an estranged soul—and it is for this very reason that they emphasize the proper funerary procedure.

5 / Ainu society

In contrast to the previous chapter's focus on the Ainu individual, this chapter will concentrate on Ainu society. It must, however, be kept in mind that the concept of Ainu society is an artificial construct, foreign to the Ainu themselves. To them, human society is only a part, albeit an integral one, of the Ainu universe in which deities, demons, and other beings live in intimate contact with humans, or *aynu*.

From the largest to the smallest, the Ainu social units comprise the entire northwest coast, the individual settlement, and the family.

THE NORTHWEST COAST

The settlements on the northwest coast are closely related to each other through kinship ties and frequent contact, thus making the entire area a functioning whole.[1] Although there are two larger ones, most settlements on the northwest coast consist of less than ten families, while those of only a few families are not uncommon. The total population of the smaller settlements scattered along the coast may be roughly estimated at about 20 families and 150 people. The largest settlement is at *Rayčiska*, which is the richest in natural resources of all the settlements of the northwest coast, with its good river, lake, and coast line. A crude estimate of the population at this settlement is about 20 families and 150 people; this is based upon my informant's description of all the families in the settlement. The next largest used to be the *Ustomonaypo* settlement. Although during the first half of the twentieth century it was reduced to three small separate settlements, it continued to be collectively referred to as the *Ustomonaypo* settlement. The total population most likely was about 15. families and 100 Ainu. In the past, according to the Ainu, some of the larger settlements, such as *Poro Kotan, Nayasi, Rayčiska,* and *Ustomonaypo,* had larger populations (see Ohnuki-Tierney 1968: 47–49), although the rest of the area has always been characterized by scattered,

---

[1] The dialect spoken by the Ainu at *Ustomonaypo* is reported to differ slightly from the one spoken at other settlements such as *Rayčiska, Hurooči,* and *Esituri* (Hattori 1957:159). However, my ethnographic data suggest that through kinship ties, economic cooperation, and so on, the *Ustomonaypo* settlement has had close contact with other settlements on the northwest coast, especially the *Hurooči* settlement.

sparsely populated settlements. My estimate of the total population of the north-west coast during the first half of the twentieth century is about 400, which is much higher than official census figures. As noted in Chapter 1, the Japanese government's surveys of the Ainu population often excluded the "remote" northwest coast, and even when the area was included they seem to have ignored those Ainu in scattered settlements (some of the census figures for the northwest coast are quoted in Ainu Bunka Hozon Taisaku Kyogikai 1970:12–15). Ainu society which is now under discussion is indeed a very small society.

The Ainu call a settlement a *kotan*, no matter what the size. Thus a *kotan* can be a large settlement such as the one at *Rayčiska* or the one at *Ustomonaypo*, in each of which there are a few clusters of houses. A "settlement" of only one house, not altogether uncommon, is also referred to as a *kotan*.

The settlements are situated along the coast, mostly but not necessarily near a river with fish. The houses are always built a short distance from the shore in a single line. There is no correlation between the location of a house within a settlement with the social status of the house's owner. As noted in Chapter 2, the Ainu used to move upstream for the winter, although at such settlements as *Opsahnaypo*, where the winter was mild, they stayed at the coastal settlement year round. The land and water adjacent to a settlement, including the mountains behind it, are usually owned collectively by the settlement, whose core members consist of male agnates. In theory, an outsider who wishes to hunt or fish within the territorial limits of a settlement must first receive permission from the chief of the settlement. However, the Ainu are not very concerned about territorial tres-passing, largely because the occupants of adjacent settlements are often relatives and, as we shall soon see, adjacent settlements depend upon each other's natural resources to a great degree. Only rarely is an important game animal in a given locale considered to belong to a particular kin group. For example, a small river called *Siripankusnay* belonged to Husko's husband's family, in the sense that only he and his close male agnates could engage in marten trapping on this river; others might catch fish or do anything else in the river but were not allowed to trap martens (see Watanabe's [1964] discussion on highly developed territorial concepts of the Saru Ainu of Hokkaido).

INDIVIDUAL SETTLEMENTS

The structures of each settlement differ considerably depending upon the size of the populations. Smaller settlements, consisting of only a few families, usually do not have a formal political structure, although they are not under the political control of larger settlements in which a formal structure exists. These small settlements are often formed to take advantage of particular food resources, such as herring runs. When the herring, for example, cease to come to the shore, the settlement may then dissolve. This is why there are many places in which settle-ments were once located, now called *oha kotan* (empty settlement).

In larger settlements, there are usually three official positions: chief (*kotan koro nispa*), vice-chief (*hačiko kotan koro nispa*), and official messenger (*sonko-*

koro aynu). The messenger goes to related settlements in order to announce significant events such as weddings and funerals. In addition to the chief, sometimes there is another official called *kotan aysara kamuy* (holy chief). He is always an extremely revered elder and therefore is called *kamuy* (deity) out of respect. When a chief is a revered elder, he may be both chief and holy chief at the same time.

Change of chieftainship takes place when a chief dies, when he retires because of old age, or when he wishes to resign to devote more time to fishing and hunting. The election of a new chief is done rather informally. Among those who are involved in the decision are the outgoing chief, if he is still alive, the vice-chief, the messenger, and the other important male elders of the community. Individuals who have a claim to the chieftainship are, in the following order, the former chief's oldest son, his younger sons, a close male agnatic kin. However, the successor must be capable of handling the job, since, as the Ainu say, "A settlement without a good chief is like a deserted settlement." Thus it is not uncommon for the chieftainship to be given to a man who is not related to the former chief through kinship, and a man from a related settlement may be appointed if he is considered to be best suited for the job. For example, when Henčo:ka, chief of the *Rayčiska* settlement, committed suicide, the people in the settlement invited a son of his father's sister (who was my informant Husko's brother), then living at the nearby settlement of *Otasuh*. He declined the offer, knowing that he was still young and that there were older and more able men at *Rayčiska*. Thus Husko's husband, No:topa Aynu, who was not consanguineally related to the deceased chief, succeeded to the chieftainship.

A chief must be a wise man who is well versed in the Ainu way of life. His personality is also important. Most of all he must be generous in sharing what he has, in this way taking good care of his people. He is usually a wealthy man who often can afford more than one wife, or can almost annually host a bear ceremony, which is an expensive undertaking. There are various other indexes of wealth, the most important of which are possession of a boat, sled and sled dogs, more than one storage house, and servants. Another important sign of wealth for the Ainu is a house with two hearths, called *tu unči o čise* (house with two hearths) or *poro čise* (big house). Other items of wealth include objects obtained through barter with other peoples, such as Japanese lacquerware and swords and turquoise beads from the Nanays. Thus in order to be wealthy, a man must be a good hunter and fisherman who can obtain a surplus of fur, fish oil, or other natural resources which he can then exchange for foreign goods.

There is an important dimension to the Ainu concept of wealth, which is quite different from ours. That is, most Ainu items of wealth have a religious character. Thus a house with two hearths, to the Ainu, is above all a sacred house with two seats for the Goddess (Grandmother) of the Hearth. It is also a house where many offerings to the deities are enshrined, since the primary function of imported goods is their use as offerings to the deities. Also, a wealthy man is often an able hunter who is good at capturing bear cubs for later use in the bear ceremony. Thus outside a wealthy house, a sacred bear cub is raised almost every year. All in all, a house with two hearths signifies an extremely holy house imbued with the atmosphere of the omnipresent deities. Often women are forbidden to speak loudly near these sacred houses. There were three of these houses with two hearths at *Rayčiska*, one of them belonging to the chief of the settlement. At *Huroočí* there was only one, owned by the chief, who also had a regular house, or *pon číse* (small house). An Ainu chief then represents in the Ainu mind an "ideal man," an able hunter-fisherman, a religious man, and a man of generosity who is well versed in Ainu ways. Not only is the culture hero depicted as a chief of a large Ainu settlement at the beginning of the world, but many great chiefs in the past have become legendary, and a good portion of Ainu oral tradition centers around the remarkable behavior of these chiefs (Chapter 3).

The primary role of a chief is to preside over war without and peace within. To the Ainu a *tumi*, or war, means a raid by a few armed men. Furthermore, to the Ainu of the northwest coast the term implies a conflict between one of their own settlements and a non-Ainu group, since war against other Ainu is unknown in this region (tales about intra-Ainu wars exist in the oral tradition of other Sakhalin Ainu as well as Hokkaido Ainu). Although the northwest coast was devoid of war during the first half of the twentieth century, its oral literature describes "military" expeditions to Orok settlements and attacks by Oroks on northwest coast settlements. These wars generally were undertaken to retaliate for an earlier attack by the other group, to avenge the slaying of a fellow group member, or to restore face lost through some insult. Issues such as the maintenance of peace, territorial claims, and desire for political conquest are not involved in Ainu warfare. These sporadic mutual attacks usually result in some casualties. Although women and children do not join the men in these forays, they often become victims when their settlement is attacked.

The chief's role as the keeper of "peace within" is not autocratic in nature. He simply presides over meetings during which particular judicial cases are debated by a number of people. These meetings are only infrequently held, since most conflicts are resolved by the individuals involved. Only when a matter is quite serious is a formal meeting held. Usually it consists of male elders, often including those from other settlements who are related to the defendant or the plaintiff. However, depending upon the case, the participants at a meeting vary. For example, when a case involves an affair between a woman and a married man, then those present at the meeting are exclusively elderly women. Although it is said that such hearings used to be held frequently, there was only one of these meetings during the first half of the twentieth century. We know only that the mother of the married man who was involved in the case was present at the meeting; no other information, such as the kinship affiliation of the members of this women's meeting, is available.

The most serious offense under Ainu law is homicide, for which the convicted person must pay, at least in theory, with his own life. Other crimes include adultery, theft, and falsehood. According to my data, adultery constitutes the largest percentage of crimes. The forms of punishment are essentially of two types: "capital punishment" and payment of goods. Capital punishment is meted out only to a murderer, who is buried underneath the victim in the ground; no coffin is used. For other crimes, compensation must be paid. The amount is decided during a hearing and depends upon the seriousness of the offense. The payment consists of such Ainu treasures as furs, lacquerware, swords, and imported clothing. Ostracism is never used as a form of punishment.

Essential to the proper understanding of the Ainu forms of punishment is the awareness that punishment is aimed at the soul of the guilty party. As we saw in Chapter 4, only a proper funeral guarantees the peaceful existence of the deceased in the world of the dead. Therefore, Ainu "capital punishment" not only denies the individual life in this world but also prevents the guilty person's soul from being reborn in the world of the dead Ainu—indeed an unbearable thought for any Ainu. The payment in terms of treasures also has a devastating effect on the soul of the guilty party and his family. Since treasures are offerings to the deities, their removal means that the punished person no longer possesses his former capacity to make such offerings. He thereby endangers his relationship with the deities, who control his general welfare, including his food supply.

There are several aspects of Ainu law which by their special nature provide insight into the law as a mechanism regulating Ainu society. First, the Ainu definition of murder includes any act which leads to a human death. For example, if person A verbally offends person B to such a degree that B subsequently commits suicide, then A is considered to be a murderer, and a formal trial must take place. This happened twice during the first half of the twentieth century. In both cases the crime was committed by the same man, often quick with his words. An examination of these two cases leads to a second important aspect of Ainu law, for in both cases the "murderer" was excused from punishment because he was related to the victims through kinship ties. According to Ainu law, whenever there is any form of kinship tie, even a remote one, between the victim and the guilty party, punishment even for murder is reduced, sometimes to nil when the relationship is a very close one. This means, then, that very seldom is a severe punishment carried out, since most of the Ainu on the northwest coast are related to each other through some type of kinship tie. In fact, in case after case, "after a long debate," a murderer, who usually committed the crime unintentionally or accidentally anyway, is excused from the *toysohkara*, the above-mentioned capital punishment in which the murderer is buried underneath the victim. Thus, going through my data on Ainu crimes I find that this greatly talked about *toysohkara* is actually carried out only upon "delinquent deities," namely, bears who have killed a man, as we saw in the previous chapter.

These two aspects of Ainu law seem to suggest that it is an effective built-in mechanism enhancing cooperation and peaceful co-existence among the members of society, without penalizing or eliminating undesirable members. Thus the Ainu definition of "murder" induces the members of Ainu society to cooperate and not to upset or gravely offend others, lest one may involuntarily become a murderer. The second aspect, the role of kinship ties as the mechanism of reducing punishment, almost suggests that the Ainu unconsciously find excuses not to punish their fellows, although they retain the penal code as a threatening and thus preventive measure to curtail violations of their law. The nonpunitive nature of Ainu law may originate from the fact that on the northwest coast the population is extremely small, and one's survival depends so much upon fellow Ainu that the group cannot afford not to rehabilitate offenders and keep them in the society if at all possible.

Among the Sakhalin Ainu on the eastern and southern coasts, the same form of capital punishment (*toysohkara*) is said to have been utilized (Sentoku 1929:11; Chiri 1944:50–53), while the absence of capital punishment, but the presence of mutilation, ostracism, and other forms of punishment is reported among the Hokkaido Ainu (Ainu Bunka Hozon Taisaku Kyogikai, ed. 1970:171–173).

The above discussion of Ainu law and crime must be viewed in light of the fact that the majority of social offenses and disagreements among individuals are handled without recourse to formal law. There are two primary reasons for this. First, there are many acts which are considered undesirable by the Ainu and yet do not constitute crimes under Ainu law. For example, there are several cases in my data of a child being severely injured by an adult. However, an act of violence, even homicide, when directed against a minor, does not call for capital punishment. Seldom is there even a trial for the offense. Second, most conflicts are resolved among the individuals concerned, even when an acknowledged crime is involved. Thus even the serious crime of adultery rarely leads to a formal trial. Other procedures operate both to resolve conflicts and reduce competition. One of the easiest and most expedient is the voluntary departure of one party to a dispute. As noted earlier, Husko's father left the *Rayčiska* settlement when he was not chosen heir to the prominent family there. Similarly, when one of his daughters was later clubbed to death by a local man at the *Opsahnaypo* settlement, he again moved with his family in order to alleviate the resultant ill feelings. Willingness to respond to disputes in this way further ensures that the type of formal trial discussed in the preceding section takes place only infrequently.

In addition to political leaders, who often are wealthy men in the settlement, there are ordinary Ainu and, at the bottom of the social ladder, a very limited number of servants. These last are of two types: orphans whose relatives take them in as household help until they themselves get married and become self-sufficient and those persons without any kin in or near the settlement. Those in the latter category occupy a lower status than those in the former category and are sometimes not well treated. The famous Japanese explorer Mamiya reported in 1855 that during the period of exploitation of the Ainu by the Nanays, Gilyak, and Orok, the Ainu "sold" fellow Ainu of the nonkin category to these peoples in order to pay their debts (Mamiya 1855:335). In a folktale from the northwest coast, before they set out for a war against the Oroks, two Ainu heroes from *Rayčiska* kill a servant and temper their swords with his liver (Tale 23 of Ohnuki-Tierney 1969b). These pieces of information suggest that in the past there may have been a class of people in a "slave" category, who did not have kinsmen and were therefore at the mercy of their fellow Ainu "owners." ("Slavery" is reported to have existed among the Hokkaido Ainu; see Takakura 1966:18.)

There is no occupational specialization among the Ainu; everyone must engage in economic activities. Some take up the additional task of being a shaman or a politico-religious leader, that is, a chief. Although shamans receive some goods for their services, they never seem to accumulate substantial wealth as a result of their special skill. There is only a very limited amount of bartering among the Ainu, since mutual help is a well-established practice, and the Ainu in one settlement on the northwest coast can go to another for a particular game, fish, or plant. When exchange of goods is necessary, there is a semistandard "price," for example, for a box of dried trout, a bundle of bleached nettle fiber, or a fur of a particular animal. A unique feature of Ainu economic transactions is that "price" depends upon ability to pay. Thus in bartering or in compensation for a shamanistic rite, a person with higher status and hence more wealth must pay a higher price for the same goods or service than an ordinary Ainu would have to pay. The semistandard price is therefore only a broad guideline for economic transactions.

KINSHIP AND MARRIAGE

At each of these settlements the core members are often, but not necessarily, male agnates. The family, the smallest social unit of the Ainu, is a nuclear, or not infrequently, an extended family. Most often an extended family consists of a man, his wife and children, and his parents, especially when the man is the eldest son. However, it is not infrequent that the eldest son lives elsewhere, either temporarily or permanently, and one of the other sons takes care of the parents. There is no taboo against the parents or consanguineal relatives of the man's wife residing with the family. As mentioned before, Husko spent all of her maiden days in settlements where her mother's relatives lived, since her father chose to leave Rayčiska where his agnates resided.

A man's capital possessions that cannot be divided are usually inherited by the man's eldest son, who in turn assumes the responsibility of the care of the parents. These possessions consist of such items as his house, boat, sled, and in rare cases, the right to a particular game animal in a particular locale. However, a man is rarely wealthy enough to make this inheritance rule meaningful, and not uncommonly the eldest son may leave the settlement for some reason, one of the other sons inheriting the man's house and caring for his parents in return. The largest share of a man's easily divisible possessions, such as furs, swords, and lacquerware, also goes to the eldest son, while the rest is divided equally among the sons of the man's wife or wives. Adopted children and, if there are no sons, husbands of daughters have equal rights with natural children. Again, the share which a son receives is usually minimal or nonexistent, since the Ainu rarely accumulate much wealth. The property transaction takes place either at the time of the son's marriage or at his father's death. None of the man's property is given to his wife or wives, since the care of the widow is the obligation of a son, usually the eldest. Only rarely is some of the man's property given to his daughter's husband in the form of a dowry, as discussed earlier.

A woman's property consists of such items as clothing, necklaces, earrings, loom, and kitchen utensils. These items are inherited by her daughters either at the time of their individual marriages or at the mother's death. Because a married couple usually lives in the settlements of the husband's parents, a woman's consanguineal kinsmen on either side are dispersed throughout the northwest coast, and there are no culturally enforced cooperative activities allowing formation of a cohesive unit. Although we do not know who comprise a women's meeting over a judicial case, at the time of a childbirth and on most other occasions, women available at the time gather, with the mother of a focal individual often playing an important role.

The only marriage taboos are that Ego may not marry a member of his nuclear family, or a child of his father's or his mother's sibling ("first cousin"). It is explained that the offspring resulting from the marriage of two members of a nuclear family will be deformed, and a child of a first cousin marriage will be physically weak. However, the Ainu prefer a marriage between two individuals who are already related. Therefore, marriage often takes place between two individuals of the same settlement or from two related settlements. The bear ceremony provides one of the rare opportunities for people from distant settlements to gather, and often at this ceremony a young person finds his or her mate or, more commonly, has a match arranged by his or her parents. Because of the preference for marriage between related individuals, married couples are often related to each other through distant consanguineal as well as affinal ties other than their own. For example, prior to Husko's marriage to her first husband No:topa Aynu, his sister had married Husko's half-brother (same mother and different father). Furthermore, No:topa Aynu's mother was a co-wife of Husko's father at the time of her marriage. Husko saw no kinship relation between herself and her husband, since her husband was the child of a marriage of his mother with another man, which took place long before his mother became a co-wife of Husko's father. (For the social structure of the Saru Ainu of Hokkaido and their marriage taboo between matrilineally related individuals, see Segawa and Sugiura, both in Nihon Minzokugaku Kyokai 1952: respectively, 62–70, 3–28; Seligman in Munro 1963:141–158; Sugiura and Befu 1962.)

The Ainu practice polygyny. That is, prominent males who can afford to support more than one household generally have two wives, and in some cases more than two. Quite often a man marries his first wife, called *onnemah* (old wife), by parental arrangement, subsequently marrying a co-wife, called *ponmah* (little wife), out of romantic inclination. Sometimes a man takes a co-wife or wives because of lack of offspring from the first marriage. A co-wife is clearly differentiated from a partner in an affair by two factors. First, she is formally married, albeit in a ceremony much simpler than that for the first marriage, and without a dowry. Second, as we saw earlier, the man's divisible property is equally divided among the sons of all his wives. The indivisible capital possessions discussed above, however, go to the eldest son of the first wife, even when the eldest son of a co-wife is older than the former. There is no culturally prescribed residence rule for a co-wife. In most cases, she establishes a separate household in her own settlement. Thus she may reside in the same settlement with the first wife, or she may reside elsewhere. Much less frequently two wives live under the same roof; my ethnographic data attest that in all three cases where this happened, the men were chiefs. When two wives live apart, often one household is neglected by the man while he is visiting the other.

The Ainu regard the practice of polygyny as enhancing the status of the man in the eyes of others. It is a tangible proof of his ability, just as amount of salary, occupational position, or possession of an academic degree is regarded as a concrete index of a person's ability in the United States. Polygyny is considered advantageous both for the man and for his respective families. That is, more wives usually mean more children. This in turn implies more security for the man in his later years, for a man's most reliable security during his old age is the care by his children. The custom is believed advantageous for the children also, since half-siblings are more likely to be of help in times of need than are strangers. Therefore, the norm among women's attitudes toward the custom is that it is wise for a woman to allow, and sometimes to encourage, her husband to take a second wife. Yet the norm or the ideal pattern does not necessarily accord with the feelings of the individuals involved. After praising wise wives who took this custom in stride and got along with co-wives, Husko most emphatically said that she, like most women, personally did not like the idea of sharing her husband. She also added that most women much prefer to be a first wife, although if a woman falls in love with a married man, she obviously cannot attain this position.

A brief description of two polygynous marriages should further illustrate how this system works in actuality. The man who headed the most prominent family at *Rayčiska* had two wives, who did not get along at all. The son of the co-wife was Husko's father, who was older in age than the son of this man's first wife. According to the rule, the younger man, being the eldest son of the first wife, became the heir to his prominent family. This outcome, in addition to a general conflict of interests, made Husko's father leave the settlement. He did not hold a grudge against his half-brother who became the heir, but remained hostile toward the mother. He and his family with Husko's mother thereafter lived mostly where Husko's mother's relatives resided. Only after Husko's mother died did Husko's father and his co-wife Setapekoro move to *Rayčiska*, where Husko and her husband (Setapekoro's son) resided. Husko's father himself took pride in having many wives and children. During a number of years when Husko's father was living with Setapekoro at a nearby settlement, Husko's mother had to support her family by herself. However, the two women got along well and they helped each other at childbirth. Husko herself is extremely fond of Setapekoro, who was one of her father's wives and her mother-in-law at the same time.

The psychological conflicts and the human elements involved in the practice of polygyny as described above may not be difficult for an outsider to understand. There is, however, an additional facet in the Ainu women's psychology, resulting from cultural patterning. That is, an Ainu woman would show a remarkable degree of tolerance if her husband took as a lover or co-wife a young unmarried woman or a widow younger than herself. She can more easily tolerate a younger woman, since the latter is not expected to "know better" than she does, and a single woman or a widow is perceived as lonely and in need of a man's help. This perception and the compassion it engenders reflect the difficulty of life for a mateless woman who is prohibited from hunting, fishing, and other male activities. The information about the relevance of age and marital status was gleaned from Husko's talk about her agony when her husband had an affair with a woman who was a wife of a son of Husko's father's half-brother. This woman's husband succeeded to the most prominent house ("big house") of the settlement, although not being especially capable, he was not elected chief. Husko claimed that this woman was doubly inexcusable, since she was older than Husko and had a husband.

At this time she also pointed out that a husband's affair is much worse than his taking a co-wife.

For a secondary marriage, levirate is a strongly preferred and often practiced mode. Thus a widow would usually marry her deceased husband's brother, and if one should not be available, his parallel cousin (a son of his father's brother) or another male patrilineally related to him. The Ainu reasons for this practice are: if a woman is good, the husband's family should not let go of her; and it is a joint responsibility of the family to take care of the wives of their men. Sororate, the practice of a widower marrying a sister of his deceased wife, is practiced, but much less frequently.

The broadest categories of Ainu kinsmen are *asirankore* (consanguineal kinsmen) and *munčiripehe* (affinal kin). *Asirankore* include all the known consanguineal kinsmen traced bilaterally and are divided into *so us asirankore* (close consanguines) and *tuyma no asirankore* (distant consanguines). There is no particular rule in terms of the number of generations included in these classifications. Affinal kin may also be classified into close versus distant affines. In addition, they may also be classified according to their age in relation to Ego's age, and also according to the sex of the affine: *poro munčiripehe* (an affine older than Ego) versus *pon munčiripehe* (an affine younger than Ego); *kokoho* (a male affine) versus *kosmah* (a female affine). There is no culturally prescribed behavior toward affines. Nor is there any activity which prohibits the participation of affinal kinsmen, although because of the patrilocal residence rule, patrilineally related males constitute the core members of most cooperative activities. When two individuals are related to each other both consanguineally and affinally, the Ainu inevitably point to the consanguineal tie as the relationship between the two, even when it is a distant one and the affinal relation is far more immediate. Although the children of two or more wives of the same man are classified as consanguineal relatives, the wives are regarded as strangers, or "outsiders," to each other.

Ainu kinship terminology is bilateral in nature. The terminological system of a child or a young person differentiates his father and his mother, respectively, from the male and female siblings of his parents. Thus a youth uses *a:ča* for father and *onmo* for mother. When he grows older and belongs to the aged category, he addresses and refers to his father, male siblings of his parents, and all other males in the age category of sixties to eighties by the same term. The same rule applies to the female counterparts. Therefore, except *a:ča* and *onmo*, all the kinship terms in Table 2 are also used as terms of address and reference to all people, including nonrelatives, in the same age and sex category as shown in the table. Ego's consanguineal kin may be specified by the possessive case of a personal pronoun, equivalent to "my," as in "my *henke* (father, grandfather)," whereas his affines may be specified as, for example, "my wife's father." There are no special kinship terms for affines. As noted earlier, personal names of older people are taboo to pronounce, and the Ainu resort extensively to teknonymy. That is, men in their sixties or above who are not Ego's father's father, for example, are addressed and referred to as "so-and-so's grandfather." The ages indicated in the table are only approximations. Because of the absence of the custom of counting age in years, it is not only difficult but meaningless from the Ainu point of view

TABLE 2   KINSHIP TERMS

Ainu Terms	When Used as Kinship Terms	General Usage
ekas	FaFaFa, FaMoFa, MoFaFa, MoMoFa	Males in the nineties and older
suh	FaFaMo, FaMoMo, MoFaMo, MoMoMo	Females in the nineties and older
henke	FaFa, MoFa	Males in the sixties to the eighties
ahči	FaMo, MoMo	Females in the sixties to the eighties
ačapo	FaBr, MoBr	Males in the forties and fifties, except Ego's Fa
unahpe	FaSi, MoSi	Females in the forties and fifties, except Ego's Fa
a:ča	Fa (used by children and the young)	
onmo	Mo (used by children and the young)	
yuhpo	OlBr	Males in the late teens to the thirties
nanna	OlSi	Females in the late teens to the thirties
ahkapo	YoBr	Males in the sub- and early teens
he:kopo	YoSi	Females in the sub- and early teens

Fa = father; Mo = mother; Br = brother; Si = sister; Ol = older; Yo = younger.

to determine age in exact terms. Besides the terms in the table, there are a few other alternatives which are less frequently used, such as the term *iruwah*, which may be used as a kinship term to specify the children of Ego's parents, or as affective term of address and reference for Ego's spouse, lover, or friend. An extremely old person, including Ego's great grandparent or great great grandparent, is called, regardless of sex, *kewsuhkehe* or *hohki putarikehe*. Terminologically, then, all the members of Ainu society are divided into different categories primarily on the basis of age and sex. Even sex is no longer used as a classificatory principle when the addressee has reached an extremely old age. The distinction between one's parents and their siblings of the same sex is expressed only in the diction of the young.

A brief survey of the workings of Ainu kinship indicates that its most salient feature is its basic flexibility. It is quite misleading simply to label its structure as "bilateral," "patrilineal," and so on. Bilaterality is seen in the individual's status at birth (Chapter 4), marriage exogamy, classification of kinsmen, and kinship terminology. Unilineality, on the other hand, is recognized in territoriality and inheritance rules. Thus, although a settlement collectively owns the land and water adjacent, its territory inherently belongs to the agnatic kin who comprise the core members of the settlement. Important game animals in a particular locale are sometimes even more explicitly owned by male agnates. Inheritance rules specify that the male's property be transmitted through the patrilineal line, while the property of a female goes through the matrilineal line; in both cases only members of one sex are involved—that is, father to sons and mother to daughters. A widow, who may be classified as the capital item of a male for analytical purposes, is likewise inherited by a male agnate, most often by a brother of the deceased man.

The Ainu social structure therefore may be viewed as essentially bilateral, with some tendency toward unilineality. Normally a male stays in his parents' settlement throughout his life. He and other males, most of whom are related patrilineally, form a corporate group which jointly owns the territory and some property such as a sled and dogs. They depend upon one another's help as is necessary. This framework provides the general rule in Ainu society in which the kinship provides the basic orientation of interpersonal relationships. Even more basic to these patrilineal and patrilocal rules, however, are the bilateral rules operating, as it were, at a deeper level. Therefore, if a man decides to leave his settlement because of a conflict in interpersonal relations or in search of a better place to fish and hunt, he may move to another settlement. Most often he moves to a settlement whose members consist primarily of the agnatic kin of either his mother or wife. He can take this alternative route within the kinship network with the approval of his fellow Ainu and without feeling as an outsider in the settlement of his second choice; the kinship ties between him and his relatives on his mother's side or those between his wife and her consanguineal kinsmen are almost equally well recognized. The superstructure of unilineality and the substructure of bilaterality augment each other, providing basic rules and alternatives. The Ainu social structure is complex yet flexible and thus well suited for this partially sedentary hunting-gathering people whose survival depends upon the unpredictability of obtaining natural resources.

INTERSETTLEMENT RELATIONSHIPS

The social structural rules discussed above must be regarded as the operative mechanisms of the entire Ainu society, consisting of all the semiautonomous settlements on the northwest coast with a total population of roughly 400 people. Interrelationships among these settlements now must be briefly discussed. Most fundamental to the intersettlement relationships is the extensive kinship network. One's "close consanguineal relatives" are usually found in a multitude of settlements. For example, Husko's paternal relatives resided primarily at *Rayčiska* and other southern settlements, whereas her maternal kinsmen resided at *Hurooči* and settlements north of it. Thus her kinsmen were found from the far north to the far south along the northwest coast. Since on important occasions such as weddings, funerals, and bear ceremonies relatives on both sides gather together, there are often considerable movements of people throughout the northwest coast.

Economic cooperation also ties the settlements together. For example, during herring season, bears are known to come frequently to the shore of the *Tooro* settlement to feast on the fish being dried on the poles. To go after these bears, hunters come from various settlements, including *Ustomonaypo* and the northern-most settlement of *Poro Kotan*. Likewise, for the spring seal hunt men go wherever there is ice. In these hunting activities, men from one settlement may engage in hunting by themselves in the territory belonging to another settlement, or the men may join the hunters from the latter settlement and share the catch. Also, no matter how and where they obtain the catch, it is almost always shared with the people in a settlement nearby, especially when the animal yields a great amount of meat. For example, if the men at *Hurooči* catch a seal, a reindeer, or a bear, people from *Ustomonaypo* are always invited, or the *Hurooči* Ainu bring a part of their catch to *Ustomonaypo* on a sled or simply on their shoulders. Mutual dependence and cooperation are also found in fishing, plant gathering, and even in fish smoking. Every year the Ainu from both *Hurooči* and *Ustomonaypo* smoke their trout along the upper reaches of the *Hurooči* river. Sometimes people from the more southerly settlement of *Rayčiska* join in, although the *Rayčiska* settlement is exceptionally rich in natural resources and the Ainu there do not have to depend on other settlements, except for herring. For herring, which is an important item in Ainu life, both for its oil and for its food value to humans and sled dogs, the *Rayčiska* Ainu regularly travel to the shore of the *Ustomonaypo* settlement.

In addition to the movements necessitated by economic activities, the Ainu change their residence rather frequently. Except in large and stabilized settlements such as *Rayčiska*, the Ainu seldom maintain residence in one particular settlement for any length of time. During her maiden days, namely, through a span of eighteen years, Husko and her family of orientation moved five times, residing at the following settlements: *Tomarikes, Hurooči, Opsahnaypo, Tooro,* back to *Opsahnaypo,* and back to *Hurooči.* Upon marriage she settled at *Rayčiska,* where she remained until 1944. Because of frequent contact among the people from related settlements, a legal case often involves the people from more than one settlement. Also, as we saw earlier, a person from a related settlement may even be appointed to be a chief. Therefore, although there is no formal political structure for the entire northwest coast, joint matters are smoothly carried out. In contrast, contact outside this area is very limited, although some does exist. There is a limited amount of economic cooperation with two settlements, *Kusunnay* and *Čiray,* which lie immediately south of this area. Besides the bear ceremony, shamanistic rituals facilitate some flow of communication with the outside areas. Able shamans from the east coast may be invited to the west coast or clients from the west coast may visit shamans on the east coast.

CRITERIA FOR SOCIAL RANKING

What then do the Ainu consider to be significant in themselves and in their fellow Ainu? First, we see that kinship affiliation is important to every Ainu. However, it is important in the sense that one should have many kinsmen upon whom one can depend in case of need. Affiliation with a particular descent group is not of paramount importance, since even a chief's son may not succeed his father unless he is personally qualified for the job. In this sense Ainu society is egalitarian and a person's own abilities count for more than his status in the kinship network ascribed at birth. We have seen this in the qualifications which the Ainu look for in a chief. Sex, another status to which an individual is ascribed at birth, however, is an important factor in classifying people and assigning roles. In the Ainu society, men's sphere of life is sharply differentiated from that of women, and males claim superiority over females. Women are barred from all ‚those activities which involve contact with the deities because of the polluting nature of their menstrual and parturient blood. Age is another important criterion determining one's social position. The aged are considered to be close to the deities and hence receive the respect of the young. They become the leaders in rituals and guardians of the sacred oral tradition. Although sex is a more important criterion than age in many respects, there is an intricate interplay of these two criteria in the assignment of the social position of older females, who are no longer contaminated with blood. For example, Husko's mother remembered an instance in which an aged female overturned the verdict in an accidental murder case which had been agreed upon by a body of male elders. Also, it is an old woman who is in charge of a bear cub while it is raised for a bear ceremony. Likewise, the language of the aged may be spoken by aged females, but not by young males. It seems then that the sex principle is more important while Ego is young, but during the later stages of his life, the age criterion comes to override the sex principle. We recall that the seating arrangement around the hearth in the Ainu house (Chapter 3) most succinctly expresses the relative importance of age and sex in social ranking. To a lesser degree we see its expression also in the greeting etiquette (Chapter 4).

Sex, age, wealth, and personal qualifications are criteria of ranking in many societies. Crucial in understanding social ranking within Ainu society is that these criteria are ultimately of a religious nature as far as the Ainu are concerned. The higher the individual's social position, the closer is his status to that of the deities. Aged males collectively occupy the highest position in Ainu society and therefore are regarded as closest to the deities. Of all the humans, the chiefs occupy the highest status, and they are usually aged males in command of abundant wealth to offer to the deities and in a position to properly conduct religious ceremonies. Even the forms of punishment in Ainu law must be understood in terms of Ainu beliefs concerning the soul. Therefore, in order to understand the workings of Ainu society in depth, it is now necessary to examine the Ainu belief system and its accompanying rituals.

6 / Beliefs, rituals, and world view

The previous chapters amply illustrate that the Ainu are very "religious" people. Yet the term "religious" does not accurately describe the Ainu life-style, since what we call "religion" is not a separate entity in Ainu life. Most of Ainu behavior, including even such an activity as disposing of trash, must be understood in terms of Ainu relations with their deities, demons, and other beings of the Ainu universe. The focus of this chapter, then, is these nonhuman residents of the Ainu universe and the relations of the Ainu with them.

SOUL OWNERS

The common denominator of most beings of the universe is ownership of a soul. Every Ainu, including a newborn baby, plant, and animal has a soul. So do most of the man-made objects, such as tools, kitchen utensils, and even grass mats. It is the behavior of the soul and not the appearance of its form that is of primary importance to the Ainu. When inside a person, the soul is invisible, being located "somewhere either in the head or in the heart." One manner in which it manifests its presence is in a person's strong emotions such as anger, hatred, and deep sorrow.

The soul is, however, most clearly perceived when it is outside its owner's body. Thus, when a person dreams, his soul frees itself from his sleeping body and travels to places distant in time and space. This is why in his dreams he can visit places where he has never been. By the same token, a deceased person appears in his dream, since the soul of the deceased can travel from the world of the dead to visit him in his dreams. Likewise, during a shamanistic performance, a shaman's soul travels to the world of the dead in order to snatch back the soul of a dead person, thereby reviving the dead. The departure of a soul also offers explanations for such phenomena as fainting and the aforementioned "temporary deaths," during which one's soul visits the world of the dead Ainu. While these phenomena take place due to a temporary departure of a soul from the body, the phenomenon of death is explained as being caused by a permanent departure of the soul. As noted in Chapter 4, however, the transference of the soul of a deceased person to the world of the dead and the continuance of the life of the deceased are guaranteed only when a proper funeral is given. Otherwise, the soul of a deceased person may trouble the living Ainu in order to remind them of a proper treatment yet to be given.

For the same reason, not only a deceased human but every soul-bearing being of the universe must upon its death receive a proper treatment, equivalent to a funeral. For animals which the Ainu eat, the required treatment of the corpse means a proper treatment of the bones. Thus the Ainu must place these bones at respective *keyohniusi*, which is a bone pile specifically allocated to each animal species. The bone pile is called *keyohniusi*, since, in the case of large animals, the skull has to be placed at the bone pile with a ritual pole called *keyohni* piercing the skull. The top of the pole is bifurcated so that the two branches will go through the eyeholes of the animal skull. The stem part of this pole is shaved to form the *inaw* ritual stick. The term *usi* means a pile.

The bone piles for the bears, reindeer, martens, and hares are owned jointly by a settlement and are located in the mountains near the settlement, each occupying a separate spot. The bone pile for the sea mammals, also jointly owned by the settlement, is located on a hill overlooking the sea. Being a marine bird, the bone pile for sea gulls is likewise located near the shore. One for the fish, however, is outside the individual's house near the ash pile. Even kitchen and eating utensils have their place outside the house where broken pieces, that is, the corpse, are disposed.

These rituals for the "corpse" of the soul owners are of great concern to the Ainu, since their negligence brings forth much suffering, mostly in the form of illness. These illnesses caused by estranged souls do not have localized pains but rather affect the patient with general fatigue. Furthermore, for this type of illness no usual herbs or other medicine is of use; the patient must resort to shamanism. The usual procedure is to ask a shaman to perform rites, sometimes night after night, until the shaman's spirit reveals which soul has possessed the sick person and what must be offered to the troubled soul so that it may leave the body in satisfaction. For example, suffering from chill and general fatigue, Husko once made a trip all the way to *Ma:nuy* on the east coast, where two famous Hokkaido Ainu shamanesses were visiting. These shamanesses, with the aid of Husko's description of her dreams, revealed that Husko had been possessed by the soul of a drowned Japanese whose body had been washed ashore at *Rayčiska* during the previous winter. Although her husband and others had buried the body, it was not buried sufficiently deep due to the partially frozen ground. The following spring, the body had come out and Husko saw it at a distance as it was dragged by a dog. Its soul possessed Husko, since she looked kind. The shamanesses directed that Husko and her family must offer lunch, footgear, and other necessary items for a trip, since the man was from southern Japan, where his soul must return to rest in peace. As this example indicates, there is no necessary connection between an estranged soul and the victim whom it possesses.

Among the illnesses caused by an estranged soul, there is a special kind called "sleeping punishment by an otter." When a person brings back an uninjured dead otter, some of his descendants are said to suffer from an illness whose symptom is a continuous feeling of sleepiness. When an otter seems dead but has no external cut, even when it is ready to decompose, the soul is believed to be

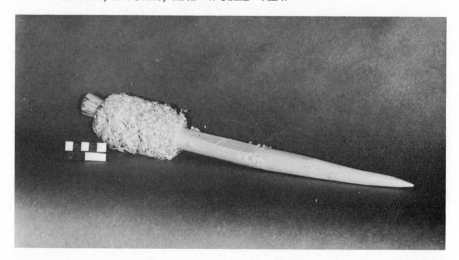

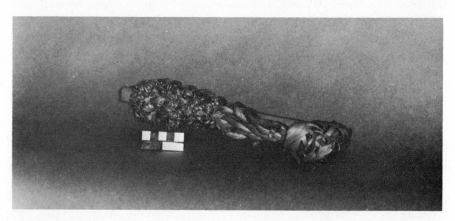

Various ritual sticks owned by Husko, 1969. (Scale 5 cm)

wandering around somewhere without leaving the body permanently. Therefore, if someone takes the body home, the soul cannot find the place to return to and causes this sleeping sickness to the person's descendants; there is no Ainu explanation why only descendants must be the victims.

The Ainu description of the soul and its behavior then seems to indicate that fundamental to the Ainu concept of soul is its free movement from the body. Only within the culturally prescribed circumstances, such as during one's dreams and temporary deaths, can it move out of its body and thereby expand, as it were, its behavioral environment. The requirement of prescribed circumstances is emphasized by the Ainu belief in possession by an estranged soul, since the soul improperly parted from its body acquires a negative power, namely, the power to cause suffering. The negative power of an estranged soul, however, must not be confused with the power which the deities and demons possess. The soul owner is not powerful by nature unless its soul is improperly estranged. Among all the soul bearers, only the deities and demons are intrinsically powerful.

DEITIES

Among the soul owners of the universe, the Ainu select a certain number of beings and deify them. Most of the important deities are classified into four groupings on the basis of the area where the Ainu believe their habitat to be. The first group comprises the deities who reside in the shore area, such as Grandmother Hearth, God of the House, and God of the Ground. The second group of deities consists primarily of nonhuman land animals and are collectively called *kimun kamuy*, or the mountain deities. Bears, wolves, foxes, owls, and what the Ainu call "mountain people" are the most important among these. The third group is *atuy kamuy*, or the sea deities, whose residence is a body of water. The two most important are the Creator of Fish, called *Čepehte Kamuy*, and a general protector called *Čo:haykuh*. They are not identified in terms of actual species of sea mammal but are believed to have the appearance of a sea mammal. The fourth group contains the sky dwellers, among whom the Goddess of Sun and Moon and the Dragon Deities are of foremost importance. There is a host of other deities, including a number of what might be called nature deities, creator deities, and guardian deities, many of which are conceived only vaguely. The Ainu also deify some of the great ancestors, and they play important roles by looking after the welfare of the Ainu. In what follows, however, I briefly describe only the most important in the Ainu pantheon.

Deities of the Shore Surpassing in her importance the other deities on the shore, *Unči Ahči* ("Fire Grandmother," or Grandmother Hearth) is perhaps only second to the bear deities in the hierarchy of the Ainu pantheon. Although the Ainu are aware of the practical benefits of fire in this north land, foremost in their minds as the image of this goddess is her "metaphysical" power with which she protects the Ainu. First of all, she is the mediator between the Ainu and all other deities at all times. Therefore, not only in formulaic prayers dedicated by male elders during major rituals but also in prayers during shamanistic rituals, one must first

address her and ask her to deliver the messages to the deities. This means that
without her help the Ainu have no way of communicating with any other deities.
Furthermore, the Ainu consider her to be a protector in an all-inclusive sense, and
they pray to her at times of emergency. The goddess is thus believed to stop a sea
storm in response to prayers by seal hunters. Likewise, a man or woman lost in
the field or mountains may ask for her help, and she somehow brings him home
safely. She even intercedes when the soul of a person is chased by a demon or
an evil spirit while he is dreaming. The Grandmother Hearth sparks in the
hearth. Her sound chases off these demons and evil spirits, and the dreamer awakes
from his nightmare. The belief may have originated from the fact that fire
frightens animals at night and thereby protects hunters.

The Ainu then must treat this goddess with extreme care and respect. One must
not soil the wooden frame of the hearth, since it is considered her pillow. While
carving by the hearth, men cannot even lay wood or tools on the frame. They
must also be careful in selecting firewood, which is regarded as the food of this
deity. The wood must be free from the contamination not only of human and animal
excreta but also from pollution by death in the family, as discussed in Chapter 4.
Not only after a death in the family but also every now and then the family must
renew the life of the goddess by renewing the ash through a special ceremony.
This ritual is called *unči yayasirikare* (rebirth of fire) and involves removing
sand and ash in the hearth and ritually disposing of them at the sacred ash pile
situated outside the house toward the east (Chapter 3). The elder of the family
then dedicates a prayer to the goddess. The women of the house fill the hearth
with fresh sand from the beach. The men must make a new pair of ritual sticks
and replace the old ones; a male and female pair of ritual sticks are always placed
at the northeastern corner of the hearth. After a new fire is kindled, the elder of
the house performs a shamanistic rite, which is followed by a special family meal.

Mountain Deities   Over and above all the deities in the Ainu pantheon, the
bears, or *iso kamuy* (*Ursus arctos collaris*), occupy the throne of the supreme
deities. Their power as deities is a generalized one, providing food and looking
after the general welfare of the Ainu. More than any other single behavior of
the Ainu, the importance placed on the bear deities is most succinctly shown in the
cultural complex of bear ceremonialism. In contrast to a simple rite which the
Ainu males perform for a bear killed in the mountains, the entire process of the
bear ceremonialism takes at least two years and consists of capturing and raising a
bear cub, the major ceremony, and the after-ceremony.

The entire event starts in the spring when men go to catch alive either a
newborn cub in the den or a cub strolling with its mother shortly after coming
out of hibernation. They capture a cub of either sex with equal enthusiasm. The
cub is called *kamuy mis* (deity-grandchild) and is regarded as a deity and a grandchild at the same time. The family of the man who captures the cub becomes the
host family. The cub is raised inside the house until its claws become too dangerous,
when it is transferred to a "bear house" or a cage outside the host's family. If the
cub is newborn and requires nursing, any woman in the settlement who is nursing
her baby will nurse the cub at the same time. (Since the introduction of dairy
farming in the recent past, cow milk was usually fed to the bear.) Although the

Libation sticks of the east coast Ainu.

Line drawing of libation sticks. (Courtesy of T. Yamamoto)

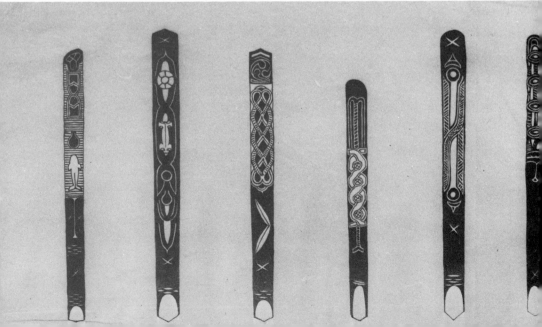

oldest woman of the host family is officially in charge of the care of the bear and plays an important role in the bear ceremony, the care of the bear is a welcome enterprise for the whole settlement, and all participate in feeding the bear with the best food even when food is not plentiful for humans. In summer they clean the cage every now and then and take the cub for a walk and bathe it along the shore. In winter they insert twigs and grasses between the logs of the cage to keep the bear warm. When the bear is pleased, it shows its satisfaction by drooping its ears, and the Ainu find it most rewarding to see this.

In the beginning of the cold season of the year following the capture of the cub, the elder of the host family holds a ceremony for the bear, which is now a year and a half in age. This major ceremony is called *kamuy oka inkara*, which means "seeing the deity off." It is held when all the preparation for the long winter is finished and when the seasonal movement was still in practice, just before they moved to the winter settlement. Most important, it must be held when the new moon first appears, that is, when the Goddess of Sun and Moon is in her best mood. Relatives and friends from settlements not only on the northwest coast but on the east coast and southern coast arrive several days before the ceremony and participate in the elaborate preparation. While all other Ainu rituals are held by individual family or by an individual shaman, the bear ceremony involves not only all the members of the settlement but those from numerous other settlements. It thus provides one of a very few occasions for people from distant settlements to gather, renewing old ties and creating new ones—the latter by the young people, sometimes leading to marriages on a later day.

On the eve of the celebration, a shamanistic rite is held to ask Grandmother Hearth to deliver the messages of the Ainu to the bear deities. All-night dancing and feasting follow this rite. At sunrise on the day of celebration, the celebrants dance around the bear cage, with a single line of men preceding one of women. The bear is taken out of the cage with extreme caution and is tied to a tree, which is bifurcated at the top and has been fashioned into a ritual stick. The bear is then decorated with many presents, made symbolically with grasses and pieces of material. The bear is believed to take these gifts back to its home in the mountains. Men and women, all dressed in their best clothes and carrying treasures, then go in single file to the altar prepared especially for the ceremony outside the house of the host. They hang their treasures on a fencelike structure at the altar. Women then must go back to their respective homes, and in the presence of men alone the elder of the host family recites a formulaic prayer to the bear deities. The prayer emphasizes the good care which the Ainu have given to the bear, their gratitude for its visit and stay with them, and their hope for more visits by the bear in the future. Just as in all the killing of animals, the purpose of the bear ceremony is to release the soul of the bear from its body so that it can go back to the mountains and renew its life there. Through this act, the Ainu ensure, or at least hope to ensure, another visit by the same bear and bears in general.

After the elder purifies the bear by waving a ritual stick over it, a specially chosen marksman, who is not a member of the host family, shoots the bear, preferably with only two metal-tipped arrows. Two choice male dogs of any color are then sacrificed as offerings to the bear deities, since dogs are considered

A bear ceremony, east coast. Photos taken by Pilsudski around 1900 (Ph NAs 701, 655 Foto-Archiv des Mf VL) and reproduced in Paproth (1970). (Courtesy of Paproth)

A Sakhalin Ainu bear ceremony. Some Ainu are wearing Japanese outfits, and Japanese spectators are in the pictures. (In Fujita 1930)

as servant-messengers of the bear deities. Women are forbidden to observe this part of the ceremony because of a belief that their presence would cause the bear to suffer longer before its death. Women are also tabooed from observing the skinning process. After the preliminary feasting in front of the altar in which both men and women participate, the cut-up meat and the hide attached to the skulls are brought into the house of the host through the sacred window. The hides are placed on the sacred side of the house toward the east and the meat is cooked in the hearth. Despite the Ainu aversion for raw food, on this special occasion some men ritually consume the bear's brain raw and drink its blood. No part of the bear's head must be consumed by women. While the bear's meat is meticulously distributed to every participant, including infants, the members of the host family must abstain from eating the meat, since they have raised the bear as their own grandchild.

After several days, when the celebration is finally completed, at dusk the elders must carry the skulls stuffed with ritual shavings, the bones of the bear and the dogs, and the bear's eyes and penis, if the bear is a male, to the special bone pile of the bears in the mountains. With that of the bear in the center and that of a dog on each side, the skulls are individually placed on bifurcated poles in the prescribed manner. This act concludes the major bear ceremony.

The entire celebration involves much merriment with drinking and eating, as well as singing and dancing, which are considered to be entertainment for the bear. The ceremony then is another example of Ainu life in which religion, recreation, and work are not compartmentalized but rather constitute different facets of a specific behavior. During the entire celebration, however, sexual intercourse of any type is forbidden. Husko remembers some individuals who were believed to have become sick or lost their minds because of their breach of this taboo. In such cases, the shamans are asked to perform rites in order to apologize to the bear deities for such misbehavior.

Some of the visitors from distant settlements stay over at the host settlement even after the celebration, not leaving until the after-ceremony, which is held at the end of the cold season (in the following year in our calendar). The after-ceremony, or *hemaka inawkara*, is seldom, if ever, introduced to outsiders, while the major ceremony has been made almost a symbol or trademark of the Ainu people. It is held during the last full moon of the cold season, traditionally in the winter settlement, by primarily the members of the host family who offer ritual sticks to the bear deities. This rite is followed by a ritual meal with the hind leg of the bear as the major dish. A hind leg, either left or right, is the only part of the bear not consumed during the major ceremony and is kept in the storage house, a natural freezer, during the cold season. Although the family members must abstain from the bear meat during the major ceremony, they must eat the hind leg, lest the bear feel sad and cry. This family rite concludes the two-year-long bear ceremonialism. It also marks the end of the stay in the winter settlement, and the Ainu move to the summer settlement and start the busy summer season during which no major rituals are held.

Since men look for cubs every spring, someone usually catches one, and at least one bear ceremony is held every year. If the settlement has more than one bear to send back to the mountains, the ceremonies are held consecutively, as it once happened at the *Rayčiska* settlement during the period dealt with in this book. If a settlement has no bear to send off in a particular year, there is usually a ceremony in another settlement to join. As a proof that a bear sent off during the ceremony is reborn in the mountains, the Ainu tell the story of a man at *Rayčiska*. This man is said to have captured a bear in the mountains with a set trap, and upon opening its skull found the very ritual shavings which he had stuffed in the brain cavity of a bear during the previous year's ceremony.

Since the Ainu bear ceremony has drawn much attention of outsiders and some of the readers may have already been introduced to the Hokkaido Ainu bear ceremony either through pictures or descriptions, the difference in their method of killing the bear must be briefly discussed. The Hokkaido Ainu use a large number of blunt arrows. Depending upon the region, the number is based on either the sex or the age of the bear. For example, the Saru Ainu use 60 arrows for a two-year-old bear and 120 for a three-year-old (Ifube 1969:36). These beautifully decorated blunt arrows are shot at the body of the bear, but not the head, before the bear is finally killed by pointed arrows. The Hokkaido Ainu then strangle the already dead or still dying bear between two logs. The whole process then gives an impression to outsiders that the Ainu are enjoying torturing the dying bear. In fact, Husko repeatedly accused the Hokkaido Ainu of great cruelty in unnecessarily prolonging the death of the bear. Husko, however, may be demonstrating an intracultural, if not cross-cultural, misunderstanding. According to the Hokkaido Ainu, the blunt arrows, which are reportedly not painful for the bear, are the presents which the bear takes home. Although I have not encountered a satisfactory explanation for the "needless" use of the two logs for strangulation, the act may have some symbolic meaning.

What we see, then, is that the Hokkaido Ainu are rejoicing over the death of the bear, not because of the "cruel" elements that we might perceive in the process but because they are able to properly send off the bear's soul with various presents from them to the bear deities, including the beautiful blunt arrows. Therefore, the Sakhalin and Hokkaido Ainu share a basic concept and attitude involved in the bear ceremony—to gracefully and properly send off the bear. (Munro's film [see "Films" at the end of this book] taken around 1930 is highly recommended as an introduction to the bear ceremony among the Hokkaido Ainu. Seligman published a useful written account of the bear ceremony filmed by Munro which she compiled from Munro's captions for the film [Seligman in Munro 1963:169–171].)

Be it the Sakhalin Ainu way or the Hokkaido Ainu way, many outsiders, like myself, may find it difficult to understand that the Ainu are unaffected by the sight of a dissected carcass of an animal. This is perhaps another reason for reports by outsiders of the "cruelty" involved in the Ainu bear ceremony. The Ainu have no qualms about killing, dissecting, and eating an animal which they have loved and respected, be it a bear, a dog, or any other animal. Although I have never observed the killing of a bear, I was quite surprised when Husko and her family killed a dog and relished eating it; I had seen them treat the dog affectionately, like a human child. From the Ainu point of view there is no contradiction in loving an animal and then slaughtering and eating it. This is partly because the Ainu regard a death as a rebirth of the soul and partly because the dissection of animals is part of their daily life, not only for the hunters but also for women and children. In fact, Husko's father taught her as a little girl about the human body functions by showing her the anatomy of a hare which he had just cut up to cook. Many of us may dissect a frog in a science class; however, our meat usually comes already cut up and wrapped in a form that does not even slightly suggest the bloody scene at the slaughterhouses.

Although overshadowed by the bear deities, wolves, foxes, and owls command respect as the mountain deities. The wolves, or *horokew kamuy* (*Canis lupus lupus*), once provided food for the Ainu, although by around 1915 they had retreated farther north. As deities they are believed to have the power to cure serious illnesses simply by appearing in a dream of the sick person or by sitting beside their own bone pile in the mountains. Because of this "tremendous power," the Ainu revere the wolves as the guardians of all the Ainu, and their sacredness forbids women to pronounce the designation *horokew kamuy* in a loud voice.

The fox, or *sumari kamuy* (*Vulpes velpes* Schrencki Kishida), is the only other animal for which the northwest coast Ainu practice the rite of capturing a cub and sending it off in a ceremony basically similar to that for the bears. The ceremony, however, is of a much reduced complexity and significance. The fox is considered the judge and arbitrator of disputes among various deities, since the animal is a fast runner and thus able to run from one deity to the other during the arbitration. There are both good and bad foxes, however, and good ones help people by issuing cries on a cliff or a hill behind the settlement to warn of a death in the near future of a kinsman residing elsewhere. Bad ones, on the other hand, trouble people by bewitchment, for which shamanistic rites are the only possible resource for cure. So that they will not be bewitched, the Ainu purposely call the fox *kiyanne kamuy* (oldest deity) to flatter him. The term *kiyanne* is used to designate the oldest person in a group, as used in "'oldest' brother" or "'oldest' woman" (among all the old women). Since advanced age is respected in Ainu society, this designation is considered a tribute to the fox deities. The Ainu also call foxes *ačapo kamuy* (uncle deities) because of the small size of the animals, although they do not explain the relationship between the size and the term "uncle." Most commonly, however, they call the deities *hu:re kamuy* (red deities) because of their color.

Owls are by far the most important birds and are considered mountain deities. The Ainu distinguish between *humse* (*Strix ualensis japonica* [Clark]) and *eturus*. *Humse* with its deep voice and large size is considered greater than other owls, of which there are several species in Sakhalin, but collectively these birds are called *eturus* by the Ainu. The Ainu emphasize that owls are beneficial in several significant ways. For example, when a bad disease is ready to spread to the settlement, an owl will cry behind the settlement, and its voice is believed to expel the disease. An owl also foretells a catch of a bear. When someone is lost in the mountains, its cry will give psychological assurance to the person, who consequently often finds his way. Because of these benefits the Ainu consider the owl as both the general guardian of the Ainu and the guardian of the settlement in particular. (For the significance of the owl deity in different regions, see Chiri 1962:196; Munro 1963:153–154.)

Besides these mountain deities which are identifiable as animal species, there is a group of deities in the mountains called *kimun aynu* (mountain people). When asked about the identity of mountain people, the Ainu explicitly state that these inhabitants of the mountains are deities and not humans, but they are not bears. One of the several tales about these mountain inhabitants is presented here.

At the *Notasam* settlement on the northwest coast, there was once a girl who went to the shore to fetch sea water for cooking and failed to come back. Some time later, people observed from a distance a girl with a birchbark container coming down to the shore to get water at *Osomapespo*, near *Notasam*. They then discovered that the print of one of her feet was that of a bear, while the print of the other foot was that of a human being, and that on the bear's footprint the inside and outside were reversed. Later two elders hid themselves behind a large rock to take a better look at the girl, whom they identified as the missing girl from *Notasam*. On being questioned by the elders, she explained that she was married to a deity in a settlement called *Hayuhsima*, and that she therefore could no longer visit where there is the smell of human beings. She promised, however, that the next time she came down for water she would take the elders to *Hayuhsima*. She instructed that when she took them to *Hayuhsima* they should not utter the word *Hayuhsima* even when they heard the voices of children and the barking of dogs as they came close to the place.

A few days later the elders met her at the shore and she led the way to *Hayuhsima*. On the way, it suddenly became so foggy that they could no longer see where they were going. They then heard the voices of children and the barking of dogs, whereupon a lake appeared in front of them. Around the lake were many houses of the deities, which were just like those of the Ainu, and the deities were wearing clothes made of marten skin. Many eagles were nesting around the lake, and their feathers were scattered on the ground. The girl had a girl and a boy with her deity-husband. As the girl suggested, the elders went home with bundles of eagle feathers on their backs.

A few days later these two men, together with a few other men, decided to visit *Hayuhsima* on their own. They again met a dense fog and heard the voices of children and the barking of dogs. At this time a fellow in the group said, "Since we can hear the voices of children and dogs' barking, *Hayuhsima* must be close by." Because of the breach of taboo by this fool, the party never found *Hayuhsima*.

In the fall of the same year, the original two elders alone decided to try to return. They made as many ritual sticks as they could carry on their backs. After a successful visit to *Hayuhsima*, they returned home with bundles of eagle feathers on their backs. Upon their return, however, the two died instantly because of a breach of a taboo. That is, whenever a human being visits a world of the deities, he must place everything he brought from the world of the deities outside the house, and then enter the house only through the smoke from a shamanistic rite. This rite is believed to eliminate a distinct smell that a human visitor to a world of the deities acquires during his stay there. When these two men returned, however, a funeral was taking place at one of their houses, and they met the funeral procession. Thus, not only were they negligent of the prescribed ritual for the returning elders but they even encountered the smell of the dead person, which is believed to be most offensive to the deities. The angered

deities killed the two men immediately. Because these men died without inform-
ing others of the location of the world of the deities, to this day nobody knows
where it is, although it is believed to be somewhere in the mountains near
Notasam.

Besides *Hayuhsima*, similar worlds of the deities are believed to exist throughout
Ainu land, but always in the mountains. No women, other than those married
to deities, are allowed even as visitors. Although it is not specifically indicated in
this story, these deified mountain dwellers are believed to be bald-headed. Therefore,
it is taboo to make fun of a bald-headed person or a person with a dermatological
disease, called *ke:čima* in Ainu, lest there occur a heavy rainfall causing a flood in
the mountains.

There are several other tales about the mountain dwellers, in all of which an
Ainu woman disappears and her footprints indicate that she is married to a deity;
one of her footprints is always that of a bear with the inside and outside of the
print reversed. Despite the Ainu's own statement that the mountain inhabitants
are not bears, the belief might have originally been a part of the Ainu belief in
the bear deities. (A similar belief in the inhabitants of the mountains among the
east coast Ainu is reported by Pilsudski [1912:135–136], although his interpretation of these figures as half human and half deity, who take the form of a bear while
visiting the Ainu, is challenged by Chiri [1944:59–60].)

Despite the ambiguous identity of the mountain dwellers, the belief as embodied
in the *Hayuhsima* story illustrates several important aspects of the Ainu notion
of the deities in general. First, they are benefactors of the Ainu. The deities offer
presents to their visitors, just as an Ainu host would to his guest. Thus, perhaps
reflecting the time when the myth was formulated, the deities are depicted as
offering eagle feathers to the Ainu visitors to take home. When the Santan trade
(Chapter 1) was at its height, the Chinese paid very high prices for eagle feathers.
The myth also illustrates that the deities' power may turn destructive. Therefore,
if the Ainu break a taboo and thereby demonstrate lack of respect, they or their
kinsmen may be killed by the very same deities who are otherwise benevolent.

Although the mountain inhabitants are pictured as "just like human beings,"
living in houses like those of the Ainu, the deities and their worlds vis-à-vis
humans and their world must clearly be differentiated. Thus, such themes as dense
fog and the smoke from a shamanistic rite may symbolize "walls" between two
types of worlds, and the whiteness of both fog and smoke may represent the ritual
purification required of a human being who traverses these two worlds. A distinction between the deities and the humans is expressed through the theme of
reversal of the inside and outside of the footprint of a deity. This theme echoes
the aforementioned reversal of day and night between the world of the deities and
that of human beings: while humans sleep, the deities are awake (Chapter 4).

Although the deities and humans as social groups of the universe must clearly
be distinguished, there are some human individuals who are transformed into
deities, such as the woman married to a deity and the two elders in the story. At
least a temporary change of status of the elders is indicated by the fact that the
Ainu must treat them like the deities and not expose them to the smell of the
dead, which is offensive to the deities.

These characteristics of the deities are not restricted to the mountain deities, as we shall see.

Sea Deities Of the deities whose residence is believed to be a body of water, two sea deities and the guardian deities of the lakes are of foremost importance. The Ainu do not deify ordinary sea mammals and fish, although they refer to the former as deities simply out of politeness. In contrast to the mountain deities, most of which are actual animals, the deities of the sea and lakes are believed not to be sea mammals but to take the form of sea mammals only when they appear to the Ainu. According to shamans and other privileged people who have extraordinary power to see things at a distance in time and space, the souls of these deities take human appearance and live in their worlds located somewhere in the sea and lakes.

Čepehte Kamuy is the producer of all the sea products, although how he produces marine resources is not explained. The appearance of this deity is only vaguely conceived, and the Ainu description of him resembles that of a harbor seal, the sea mammal of the greatest economic value to the Ainu. Since *Čepehte Kamuy* is so great as to provide not only for human beings but even for their supreme deity, that is, the bear, the Ainu pay due respect to this deity by offering ritual sticks and observing taboo behaviors, some of which were introduced earlier (Chapter 2). A shortage of fish in particular is believed to be caused by the anger of this deity. Thus, if someone carelessly throws into a bay objects which are offensive to the deity, such as a dog's skull or a snake, the deity will close the door to the exit of fish, and then the bay, once rich in fish, will suddenly be barren. The Ainu must then perform a ritual for the deity in order to appease his anger by offering prayers and ritual sticks.

Another important sea deity is *Čo:haykuh*. The Ainu description of his appearance rather closely matches that of a killer whale, although the Ainu, as mentioned earlier, believe that the true identity of the deity is not a sea mammal. Being a deity, *Čo:haykuh* may not be caught and eaten. Instead, when sea mammal hunters spot one of these deities, they must cast toward it in the sea ritual sticks and other available offerings. If it is spotted from shore, the women must refrain from relieving themselves facing the sea, and they must not even cast their eyes on it.

Despite their small size, the Ainu explain that when *Čo:haykuh* deities encounter a whale, they cut up the whale into pieces with their fins. Then they let bones and other inedible parts sink to the bottom, allowing only the boneless square chunks of meat to float to the surface so that the Ainu may enjoy the whale meat. The northwest coast Ainu did not engage in whaling but relish whale meat whenever it is available—either when the deity provides the meat in this manner, as it is said to have happened once at *Hurooči* in the recent past, or when a dead whale is washed ashore.

Čo:haykuh is also said to guard the Ainu boats when they are caught in a storm. This power was once demonstrated to the men at *Hurooči* when they met a sea storm during a spring seal hunt. Suddenly a number of *Čo:haykuh* appeared and lined up on both sides of the boat, whereupon a strip of water ahead of the boat became calm, enabling the men to return home amidst the storm without any difficulty.

The following tale symbolically expresses the beneficial role of the deity perceived by the Ainu.

A long time ago at *Yohohkinay* near the Russo-Japanese border there was an elderly couple who had a very good-looking daughter. She always adorned herself with beautiful pieces of jewelry. Numerous suitors, from her settlement as well as from afar, courted her without any luck. The people in the settlement began to gossip, "She is very snobbish. If she thinks she is so precious, why doesn't she marry a deity!" One day her father made a number of ritual sticks from freshly cut willow branches and asked his daughter to accompany him to the shore. As they sat down next to each other, he asked her to take lice out of his hair. He then explained to her what the people in the settlement said of her and asked her if he could marry her to a *Čo:haykuh*. She agreed. They went back home in order to decorate her with golden earrings and numerous other ornaments. As they returned to the shore, the father covered the floor of his boat with ritual sticks and had her sit on them. He placed more ritual sticks, food for offering, and all the family treasures from home in the boat so that it looked like an altar, and she looked as beautiful as a goddess. As the father rowed the boat away from shore, three sea deities appeared and headed toward the boat. They looked like small whales without spout holes, but instead having a dorsal fin. The one in the middle was the *Čo:haykuh* whom the daughter was to marry, and the two on the sides were his servants. As the three came next to the boat, the father put the ritual sticks and offering dishes along with his daughter on the back of the master *Čo:haykuh*. He then hung his sword, which was his most precious treasure, from his daughter's shoulder and put the rest of the offering dishes on the backs of the servants. The three circled around the boat and swam offshore. The father headed home only after he saw the three deities and his daughter disappear on the horizon.

Beginning the next day the man and his wife daily found a great amount of fish on the shore in front of their house. The fish were even placed on *mačahči* grass (a plant used by the Ainu to wrap fish in or place fish upon) and were as fresh as if they had just been caught. In other words, the *Čo:haykuh* whom their daughter married served his parents-in-law as would any good son-in-law (Chapter 5).

A few years later the man again loaded his boat with ritual sticks and offering dishes and set out from shore. The deity appeared with his daughter, who was carrying a baby. The father and the daughter embraced each other. After the father placed ritual sticks and offering dishes, the three swam off.

The Ainu, who consider themselves to be related to this couple at *Yohohkinay*, regard this story as a concrete example that *Čo:haykuh* as the guardian deities look after the welfare of the Ainu. The tale also demonstrates how the *Čo:haykuh* taught some of the customs which the Ainu now observe. At the time when the daughter appeared to her father after being married to the *Čo:haykuh*, she was clothed in a garment with a mandarin collar. The idea of a type of women's garment with a mandarin collar is thus said to have been given to the Ainu by this woman. Furthermore, her baby had a triangular piece of material hanging from his hair in front of his forehead, and he originated the aforementioned hair style of Ainu male children (Chapter 4). (For further analysis of the tale, see Ohnuki-Tierney 1968:245–247.)

The extreme sacredness of both *Čepehte Kamuy* and *Čo:haykuh* commands that no one, especially women, pronounce their names above a whisper. Furthermore, when anyone starts talking about either one of the deities, he must preface his remarks with the address *"Reporo un kamuy henke utah"* (the deity-elder offshore). This taboo requiring that their names not be uttered out loud is applicable to all important deities as well as revered elders. However, the taboo is most rigorously observed in reference to these two deities. Husko was perturbed when, carried away in my conversation, I pronounced their names in the normal volume of my voice, although she never reprimanded me when I mentioned aloud names of other deities, including the bears.

Another group of important deities whose residence is a body of water are the guardian deities of lakes. Each lake is believed to have its guardian deity, who usually appears to the ordinary Ainu in the form of a harbor seal, but sometimes as a big *čiray* trout; only shamans and other sagacious Ainu can tell that the creatures are deities and not ordinary seals or trout. They can be either male or female. For example, the lake at *Rayčiska* had a female guardian deity who appeared as a small harbor seal, and was thus referred to as *to: ahči* (Grandmother of the Lake). At another lake at *Arutoro* near *Rayčiska* the guardian was a male *čiray* trout, which was "so large that it looked like a house upside down." Most of the Ainu, however, have never seen these deities. Their presence is identified primarily by their voice. They inform the Ainu just before something undesirable, such as a drowning or storm on the lake, takes place. Again a tale most vividly illustrates the Ainu belief in this category of deities.

Long ago there was a man who lived with his wife in a settlement on the shore. When the husband returned with game from his daily hunt, his wife cooked the meat. They ate and slept together. One day after the man went hunting, the wife cooked an offering dish, placed the food in a red bowl on a red tray, and dressed herself in fine clothes and jewelry. With a ceremonial grass mat and the offering dish on her arms, she followed a meandering road which started behind her house. When she arrived at a small lake, she put the mat at the edge of the lake, placed the offering dish on the tray, and danced. While dancing, she called to the guardian deity of the lake, "Come up quickly. Let us make love day and night." As she continued to dance, she saw a seal emerging from the middle of the lake. As it arrived at the shore and shook water off its body, it transformed itself into a good-looking young man. The two made love day and night, and the deity ate the offering dish. She then was reminded that she should go home before her husband returned from the mountains.

Upon her return home, she changed to her daily clothes and cooked a meal for her husband. They continued their daily life as usual. After a few days, her husband again left for the mountains and she for the lake. She again had an enjoyable time with the deity and came back home in time for her husband's return. Again after a few days, the two headed for the mountains and the lake, respectively. This time the deity even left a small amount of the offering dish for her to eat (as we saw earlier, this is the Ainu way of proposing). While they were enjoying themselves, however, the deity all of a sudden groaned and writhed in pain. She then saw her husband, who she thought was hunting, standing in front of her. The deity was bleeding from the wound caused by her husband's harpoon head. The deity fled to the lake while her husband beat her.

At home the husband did not speak to her. She, on the other hand, could not help thinking about her deity who was wounded because of her. Finally she made an offering dish, dressed in her best, and went to the lake. At the lake the blood of the wounded deity was still visible, and following the trail, she was led under the water and up on the opposite shore of the lake. There stood a huge rock which housed a large cave, from which she heard the sound of someone groaning. She coughed several times to notify the host of her visit. A young woman, who was the sister of the deity, came out and led the woman into the cave. The deity was groaning and writhing, with his head on an elevated pillow and his feet on another elevated pillow. She took care of the deity until his wound was completely healed. A few years later she gave birth to a boy and a girl. She reached old age and upon her death she joined the world of the deities. There she heard that her children had become famous (for details, see Tale 7 of Ohnuki-Tierney 1969b).

Sky Deities Before discussing the deities of the sky, I must first briefly outline the Ainu concept of the sky, which is entirely different from ours. The Ainu state that the *kanto,* which is at least partially equivalent to our common notion of sky, consists of "six" layers. Since the number six in Ainu denotes "many," we may visualize the Ainu vertical sphere as somewhat like a layer cake, although whether or not the entire shape of the universe is cubical, domelike, or delineated at all is not clear; the Ainu statements on the spatial configuration are confined to the "six"-layer structure. Each layer of the sky, according to the Ainu, consists of a layer of ground, a layer of sky, and the space between. Despite the multilayer concept of the atmosphere, however, in terms of daily perception of their behavioral environment, the Ainu live in a reality in which there is the ground on which they live, the space between the ground and the sky, and the sky, on top of which there is another layer of ground on which the deities of the sky reside. The most important of these deities are the Goddess of Sun and Moon and the dragon deities, although numerous other deities as well as such creatures as hares, musk deer, and worms are believed to reside on the ground in the sky.

The sun, or *to:no čuh* (daytime moon), and the moon, or *kunne čuh* (dark moon), are considered the same female deity, who is the most important of all sky deities. Just like the Grandmother Hearth, another female deity in the Ainu pantheon, the Goddess of Sun and Moon, or *Čuh Kamuy,* mediates between the Ainu and other deities. Therefore, as we saw earlier, no Ainu ritual may be held during the latter half of the month when the deity is believed to be crying and hence not able to deliver Ainu messages. Each household performs a special ritual for the goddess twice a year, for which they erect a special ritual stick outside the house. Carved on this ritual stick is the representation of the six layers of the sky, made by peeling three horizontal strips of bark from the tree trunk; the six alternating bands of the peeled and unpeeled bark symbolize the six layers of the sky. Since the deity is a female, the Ainu also make two wooden circular rings and attach them to the ritual stick as her earrings. Although she is referred to as *kanto koro kamuy* (deity who possesses the sky), the Ainu offer no specification on the nature of the power of this goddess other than her role as a mediator. Other celestial beings are not under her control, and natural phenomena related to the sky, such as wind and storms, are not ascribed to her doings. Solar and lunar eclipses are considered to constitute the same phenomenon, and they are believed to take place when either a crow, fox, squirrel, or octopus swallows the goddess.

The dragon deities, or *Kanna Kamuy,* are another important group of sky deities. Although their residence is somewhere in the sky, they sometimes come down to rivers and lakes to drink water or just for a visit. They are believed to engage in periodical fights among themselves, and thunder is considered to reflect the sound of the fighting and lightning, the flashing of swords. The Ainu have no explanation for why the dragon deities are beneficial, nor do they perform any ceremony for these deities, yet they consider them most sacred and powerful. Thus they may not keep for a prolonged period of time any pictorial representation of a dragon, such as an imported Chinese garment with an embroidered dragon on it, just as they cannot keep bear hides.

The existence of the dragons is real to the Ainu, as testified in several tales. For example, not too long ago at *Tomarikes* on the northwest coast, there was a great thunderstorm during which many live rabbits and vipers, some of which had been halved, fell from the sky. Then suddenly a huge object fell from the sky and blocked the entire mouth of the bay at *Tomarikes*. It was a dragon deity. Although no one else knew what to do, a sagacious old woman told the people to stay inside, and she alone went to the top of a high cliff next to the bay. There she prayed to the dragon deity while waving her underwear, whereupon the deity climbed the cliff and ascended to the sky. The traces of his claws on this cliff are still vividly seen as if the incident took place only a short while ago. Because of this incident, the place is named *Kamuy Intara* (deity's footprints).

Although many deities are believed to dislike sewing needles, the dragon deities are most sensitive to as well as afraid of needles. Thus, as a tale goes, there once was a very good-looking Ainu woman whom a handsome and well-dressed young man started to visit nightly. After a short while they were married. The man had a human appearance when sleeping with the woman. However, one day the woman happened to see him as he was leaving the house, and it was hard to tell whether he was a deity or a demon. She then realized that her husband was a dragon deity who had been visiting the lake behind the settlement. Being afraid of him, she secretly inserted a needle in his garment when he returned. He went out again the next day but never came back. She went to the lake, where she found a dead dragon deity with a needle stuck in his body.

This story illustrates a curious departure from the Ainu attitude toward deities. The Ainu kill other deities only to ensure the rebirth of their souls, or only when a deity threatens Ainu well-being—for example, when a deity snatches a wife from an Ainu male, as in the previous story. In this dragon tale, however, a dragon is killed by the woman herself simply because of her fear of the dragon deities. The lack of any ritual for these deities other than the taboo, this departure from traditional Ainu attitude, and several other factors suggest to me that the belief in the dragons may have been introduced not long ago by some other peoples on the Asian continent, where the belief in dragons has an extremely long history.

Concept of Deities   Although the northwest coast Ainu pantheon includes many more deities than those discussed above, the Ainu are restrictive in deifying the beings of their universe; they select a relatively small number of beings as their deities. My realization of this fact came, unfortunately indeed, only very slowly as I first misunderstood the Ainu use of the term *kamuy* (deity or deities). I copied down all the beings the Ainu referred to as *kamuy* and included them in the Ainu pantheon until I went through my list of deities one by one in order to seek the "native" explanation of why each one is deified. My conversation with Husko went something like the following. "Why are the hares *kamuy?*" "Why in the world are they *kamuy?* Even women can just catch them and eat them." "But you have been referring to them as *osukeh kamuy* [hare deities]." "Oh well, it is always good to call any being politely as *kamuy.* Then its soul would be pleased and won't do any harm to us. That is why we call even demons *kunne kamuy* [dark deities, or the deities of the dark] or *wen kamuy* [evil deities]. Then, they will be pleased and stay away from us. If we call them demons, they will be insulted and attack us." Consequently, those beings crossed off my list of bona fide deities included several economically important land and sea mammals, several birds, grasshoppers, and snakes, as well as such objects as talismans, amulets, and tools.

My inquiry into the Ainu concept of deities was further complicated by another use of the term *kamuy.* That is, when the term is used alone rather than with a specification, as in *sumari kamuy* (fox deity), it can mean either a generalized notion of *kamuy* (deities in general), specifically bears which are the supreme deities, or a particular deity which is being discussed at that time. Needless to say, after I came to realize these usages of the term *kamuy,* I had to spend many hours going over my field notes, which were written without real understanding of the Ainu concept of the deities.

Who or what then are the Ainu deities? It is noteworthy that the Ainu pantheon is not equal to nature, nor are all the beneficial beings of the universe Ainu deities. Thus, ordinary seals, which are most useful for the Ainu as providers of meat, hide, and oil, are not deified; *Čepehte Kamuy* (the creator of marine resources) is not a seal but only looks like a seal. Neither are such economically important beings of the universe as plants, fish, dogs, musk deer, and reindeer deified. On the other hand, wolves and foxes, which offer very limited economic value, are important deities. Briefly considering some of the deities, I try to decipher, in the following discussion, the Ainu concept of deities. What follows, then, does not represent the Ainu interpretation and generalizations of their pantheon but my attempt to understand why the Ainu choose certain beings of their universe and deify them. For this purpose I pieced together what the Ainu have to say about each of the deities, presented above, what I know of the nature and behaviors of these beings, and what they perhaps mean to the Ainu.

First, Grandmother Hearth. Although her role as the mediator predominates in the Ainu mind, the practical importance of fire needs no reiteration. In this north land, even in midsummer, the fire in the hearth must be kept going. In addition, the only way the Ainu can transform raw food, which they detest, into edible food is by the heat of the hearth. Fire also provides one of the few methods of food preservation; in addition to drying fish in the sun and freezing it naturally, the Ainu smoke a great quantity of fish for winter supply. Light from the hearth and light from the shell lamp kindled from the fire in the hearth provide the only light at night when men and women do their woodworking, weaving, and sewing or sometimes just listen to tales. For the hunters, Grandmother Hearth provides not only warmth and cooking heat but the only real protection from animals during their stay in the mountains. Yet the Ainu are well aware of the destructive power of fire once it is out of control.

Like fire, bears are beneficial to the Ainu as a source of meat and oil. Yet they can easily kill human beings. Bears have the enigmatic behavior of hibernation—being able to survive during the entire winter without eating and drinking, as well as, in the case of females, even bearing offspring and nursing them—which is totally beyond the ability of human beings whose great portion of labor during the summer is spent for winter survival. Wolves and foxes are seen as super-intelligent animals, and the former can even kill such large animals as reindeer. Owls positively help the Ainu by eating mice and rats, which are a real menace, threatening as they do human survival by attacking the winter supply of food in the storage house. Owls are also mysterious—they are not only unique among birds in having humanlike faces with their eyes in the front but they fly without sound and stay awake during the night. Therefore, the waking hours of owls actually fall into the portion of time which the Ainu allocate to the deities and demons.

The importance of the sun and moon needs little explanation. However, I might point out that the warmth and brightness of the sun are more appreciated in this north land than in more southerly areas. Also, the moon provides the only source of light outside at night and thereby saves the lives of people who must walk at night. Also, drying of fish in the sun is an important means of food preservation, as seen earlier. The Ainu do not link the two sea deities to what we call fauna or natural phenomena, although we may suspect that originally seals and killer whales, respectively, have given rise to the formation of these "mythical" deities. They are beneficial to the Ainu in producing fish and providing whale meat, both of which are done because of the superhuman power of these deities. To the dragon deities the Ainu assign only dangerous powers of being able to cause thunder and lightning; they have no specific power which is beneficial to the Ainu. The dragons are mysterious beings of the universe, having the properties of creatures living in different parts of the universe, such as the wings of a bird, the scales of a fish, and the head of a horse.

It seems, then, that the most important property of the beings which the Ainu choose to deify is a special quality which exceeds human capabilities. Most of the Ainu deities are at the same time beneficial to human beings. The greater the deity, the more general is its power, as in the case of bears and "killer whales." The Ainu do not deify, as they explain, "plants and animals which we can easily catch and eat, and which cannot do any harm or good to the Ainu." To their selected beings the Ainu ascribe additional "metaphysical" powers, such as the role of mediator to fire, and it is these powers that become the most important quality the Ainu associate with their deities. Therefore, Grandmother Hearth is most important as the mediator, and fire as the source of heat and light stays almost in the background in the Ainu mind.

The Ainu are, however, also respectful to all soul bearers. This courtesy toward a soul is often indistinguishable from their reverence for what they call "real deities." Crucial, however, is the fact that the Ainu perform a specific ritual for each of the bona fide deities, while their ritual for ordinary soul bearers is restricted to a proper care of the soul.

The concept of Ainu deities just outlined differs significantly from many interpretations of the Ainu deities by other scholars, most of whom worked with the

Hokkaido Ainu. Many of them define the Ainu deities more broadly. For example, Watanabe equates the *kamui* [*sic*] with all nature (1964:81), while Chiri includes plants and objects such as boats and anchors among the *kamuy* (Chiri 1954:359). Kindaichi includes an equally wide range of phenomena in the *kamui* [*sic*] class (1925:253–258). The differences in interpretation of Ainu deities should perhaps be largely attributed to regional differences and to changes in Ainu concepts over time. It would be interesting to find out if Ainu in other regions have an equally generous use of the term *kamuy* and also refer to nondeified beings as *kamuy*.

As the last topic of the Ainu deities, Chiri's intriguing suggestion may be briefly discussed. Chiri states that all the animal deities of the Ainu are actually human beings in appearance and live as humans when in their own country. However, they disguise themselves when visiting the Ainu world, since they wish to bring meat and fur as presents to the Ainu, just as any Ainu guest would come with a gift (Chiri 1944:27–28; 1954:359–361). When asked directly if this is the case, the Ainu on the northwest coast reject the idea. However, several of their tales, such as those about the bald-headed mountain deities, *Čo:haykuh* (killer whale), and the guardian deity of a lake suggest that the Ainu picture these deities as having a human appearance and life-style when they are in their own worlds. It might be that the Ainu in the regions of Chiri's investigation spelled out their perception in this respect more clearly than the Ainu of the northwest coast of southern Sakhalin.

DEMONS

The presence of demons, or *oyasi*, is as real to the Ainu as that of deities. Representing a concept which is a polar opposite of that of the deities, the demons signify the intrinsic power to endanger and often kill human beings. Consequently, the most dreadful demons are those which have the power to exterminate the total population of a settlement, such as the husband and wife demons which the culture hero *Yayresu:po* killed at the beginning of the universe. In this tale *Yayresu:po* is described as the sole survivor of two adjacent settlements which had been exterminated by the demon couple with one eye, which was as large as a full moon. In order to raise the culture hero, then a small baby crying in the deserted settlement, his guardian deity descended from the sky. When the boy became a young man, the deity revealed his identity. He then clothed the boy for war, and after instructing him how to kill the demons, the deity demanded that the boy kill him so that he (his soul) could go back to the sky. Unwillingly, but urged by the deity's strong demand, the boy finally summoned his courage and killed the deity, whose soul subsequently traveled to the sky amidst the sound of a shamanistic rite and the deity's voice (the deity is presumably performing the rite).

The boy then made his lunch of dried trout and, following the directions given by the deity, reached the male demon's den, in front of which there was nothing but a pile of human bones. Smelling human flesh, the demon came out. His one eye was as large as a full moon, and his upper jaw touched the sky, while the lower jaw dug into the ground. Since his skin was impenetrable, the boy jumped into his mouth, and with a sword given by the deity, he ripped the stomach of the demon to pieces from the inside, thereby killing it. After he sliced the flesh of the demon and distributed its meat to the trees, grasses, ground, rivers, and all other beings of the universe, he set forth to kill the female demon. With aid from a female deity, who disguised herself as an elderly woman, he killed the female demon in a similar manner. He then repopulated these two settlements by bringing people from elsewhere.

There are numerous other demons, the more "famous" ones having been present at the beginning of the universe, and these are described only in myths (see Ohnuki-Tierney 1969b). Some are only vaguely conceived. Others are perceived without particular appearance and may be referred to as evil spirits in our phraseology. All of them, however, are referred to as *oyasi*, of which the Ainu themselves recognize two types: visible and invisible. They can be assured of the presence of the invisible demons when they are in the vicinity of one, since they will feel a strange sensation. Besides these "native" categories, I see another way of classifying the Ainu demons into two types: intrinsic demons and estranged-soul demons. The intrinsic demons are those born demons, as it were. Some of them are what we may call "imaginary," such as the demon couple introduced above, while some correspond to actual fauna of which the Ainu have very little factual knowledge. For example, lynx (Chapter 2) have been so few in number in southern Sakhalin that the Ainu associate them primarily with the "mythical" behavior of the animal, such as being able to multiply instantaneously. Another example would be the demon birds (perhaps nocturnal birds belonging to *Caprimulgidae*), whose voices are believed to cause insanity or "raise a house upside down." Since they are nocturnal birds, the Ainu have little knowledge of their identity except for the sounds heard at night. Yet some other intrinsic demons are stray members of ordinary species, such as rats. A stray rat then takes on unusual behavior, such as invisibility or gigantic size. What I call estranged-soul demons, on the other hand, represent an entirely different type of demon, in that they are not demons by nature but turn into demons because of Ainu maltreatment of their souls. Among these are the musical instrument demons (Chapter 3) and Ainu tools which turn into demons when they are left behind intact when, for example, the owner moves to another settlement. Therefore, it is essential that the owner break all the tools he cannot take along so that their souls will be able to detach themselves and properly join the world of their dead members.

The Ainu rituals for demons focus on either warding them off or killing them as well as preventing the rebirth of their souls. In order to keep the demons away, various preventive measures are taken, such as wearing charms and amulets and, as we saw in Chapter 4, clothing an infant in rags or calling him with a "dirty" name. As prevention against a spreading disease, which is believed to be caused by demons and evil spirits, the Ainu place various charms against the doorway and plant puppy skulls, grass bundles, and carved sticks on the roadside. It is believed that the puppy skulls come to life and bark at the demons and that the grass bundles become warriors who fight the demons with sticks which have turned into swords. There are numerous other ritual behaviors, including various exorcism rites such as those performed in connection with funerals (Chapter 4).

The Ainu ritual for preventing the rebirth of a demon's soul requires the distribution of the slain demon's body to the beings of the universe for consumption. Thus, in contrast to the Ainu ritual to ensure the rebirth of deities and soul-bearing beings, the Ainu rituals for demons focus on exterminating a demon's soul as well as its body.

RELATIONS AMONG DEITIES, DEMONS, AND HUMAN BEINGS

The above description just given of the Ainu deities and demons reveals only a very small part of the highly complex universe of the Ainu, in which the deities, demons, and human beings constitute the three most important social groups. The deities are powerful but benevolent, the demons are destructively powerful, and the human beings are powerless against either the deities or the demons. Much of Ainu behavior is governed by efforts to please the deities and ward off the demons. The "communication" between these three types of beings of the universe takes many forms. To the deities, the Ainu convey their respect and other messages by performing rituals and observing various taboos, the violation of which will offend the deities. The deities respond, if pleased, by granting the Ainu abundant food, children, general welfare, and the knowledge and skills to cope with life. However, if offended, the deities punish the Ainu with death, illness, famine, and so on.

In addition to such communication, the deities and the Ainu exchange members. Thus, a deity may marry an Ainu woman and live temporarily in the Ainu world or visit the Ainu world to give aid, as described in the culture hero story. Conversely, an Ainu male can visit the world of the deities, or an Ainu female can marry a deity, who in turn does favors either for her kinsmen or for the Ainu in general. In certain instances, an Ainu may be deified after death; thereby he forsakes his membership in the human world and joins the deities.

Another type of communication between the Ainu and deities involves demons. In order to tackle the most dreadful demons, the Ainu must receive help from the deities. Somehow the Ainu deities never slay the demons themselves, but simply provide the Ainu with instructions as to how to kill them. Therefore, not only must the Ainu seek positive favors from the deities, but they must also seek protection from the demons.

However, some of these most dreadful demons are simply soul-owning beings of the universe which have turned into demons because of Ainu maltreatment. Furthermore, even benevolent deities can be lethal if the Ainu misbehave.

What we see, then, is that the power to turn any beings of the universe into either a benevolent or malevolent elements rests in the hands of the Ainu, who, in Ainu theory, are powerless. In addition, this ability of the Ainu to form and transform the nature of the beings of the universe gives an amazing fluidity in the basic scheme of classification of the inhabitants of the universe; a member of one social group can transfer to another.

SHAMANISM

Shamanism or *tusu* is an important and integral part of Ainu religion. However, it contrasts to other practices of Ainu beliefs and rituals in several significant ways. These contrasts serve to elucidate the nature of shamanism, and hence its discussion is presented in the last section of this chapter.

There are strict rules as to when and where a shamanistic rite may be performed. The time is after sunset, never during the daytime. The embers from the hearth provide the only light. A rite may be performed at any time of the year. In actual practice, more rites are held during winter when the Ainu are less busy than during the summer fishing season. The location is always inside the house beside the hearth. Finally, a menstruating female may never be present, either as a shaman or as a member of the audience.

Although there is no official announcement of the performance, the people interested gather at the shaman's house as they hear the shaman's drum, with which he initiates his performance. To produce smoke, the shaman's assistant places three aromatic plants on the embers: a branch or two of Yesso spruce or, if the shaman is a woman, of larch, a plant belonging to genus *Ledum* called *nuhča*, and minced dried leeks. Throughout the rite the shaman drinks sea water from a bowl in which the aforementioned Yesso spruce and *nuhča* as well as a piece of kelp (seaweed) have been soaked. Although the Ainu consider the solution too salty for human consumption, a shaman often consumes two or three bowls of it during a rite, since it is supposedly the spirit helper, not he, who drinks it. The solution is also used at the beginning and the end of the performance when the shaman exorcises evil spirits by spraying it from his mouth.

The shaman commences the rite by asking Grandmother Hearth and other deities for help. He then presents the specific case for which the rite is being performed, for example, describing the symptoms of his client's illness. Amid the smoke from the plants and the sound of drumming, and helped by the salty solution, the shaman becomes possessed by his spirit and reaches a state of at least semitrance or semiunconsciousness (a very small amount of paracresol in the plant *nuhča* or alkaloid in the aconite roots consumed by some shamans [see later] might have some effect on the shaman). His voice becomes harsh and different from his normal one. He produces strange sounds, including whistling and groans and rapid oral utterances like "ya, ya, ya. . . ." The most important part of the rite occurs when his spirit helper relates, through the shaman, the message received from a deity, for example, concerning the cause and mode of cure of an illness. Since the deity's messages usually involve both the language of the deities and that of the aged discussed earlier, there must be a person in the audience who deciphers the messages for the "general public," that is, the audience. This is necessary, since many shamans claim that they do not remember what they have uttered during the performance.

The drum is an important element in Sakhalin Ainu shamanistic rites. It functions both as a charm against evil spirits and as a means of summoning spirit helpers and calling the attention of the deities. The continuous and rhythmic sounds of the drum in the dark, in a small house, usually crowded with people, often have an unusual effect on both the audience and the shaman. Shamans do not wear special garments for the performance, and their paraphernalia include only a

Husko, with her drum and ritual shavings for shamanistic rites on the wall (left). Her amulet and ritual shavings are on the wall to the right. (Taken in the 1950s) (Courtesy of Husko)

special headdress, a headband to which various charms are attached, a necklace, and ritual shavings.

In the majority of cases, the rites are performed in order to seek from the deities information about the cause of an illness and its cure. The illnesses for which the rites are performed are serious ones, which the Ainu call *araka*. The *araka* are differentiated from minor discomforts involving localized aches and pains, although extraordinary burns and cuts are classified as *araka*. Common causes for serious diseases include the wrath of the deities caused by improper behavior on the part of the sick person, or more often another human; bewitchment by a fox deity; and possession by an estranged soul. Most often there is no necessary connection between the sick person and the particular cause of the sickness. Rites may also be held to locate either missing persons or objects, or to seek advice from the deities in naming a child. Some shamans are noted for miracle performances. For example, a shaman may revive a dead bear or a deceased human being, presumably by going to the world of the dead to fetch back the departed soul. Other examples include driving a knife into his chest without harming himself and miraculously materializing the sea and walking on it with a cane. Most of the reported miracles were performed by shamans now long deceased. A more common type of "miracle" performance is the consumption of aconite roots, whose alkaloid poison can be lethal. It is explained that it is the particular spirit helper which likes aconite roots rather than the shaman that consumes the root, and hence the shaman is unharmed. (There are several species of aconite in Sakhalin, and some shamans possibly know and use nonlethal varieties.) Whether in legends or in actuality, these miracle performances serve to reinforce the belief in shamanistic power.

When the shamans fail to produce the anticipated result, as it happens at times, they advance a number of circumstantial reasons to explain their failures. For example, a menstruating woman supposedly in the audience is blamed for preventing good deities from coming to help.

Despite occasional failure, however, shamanism seems to provide a great deal of psychological relief and reassurance to the patients and thereby an actual improvement of their health. For this reason a shaman himself often performs a rite when he is not feeling well. Husko, for example, often told me that she was feeling better because she had performed a rite the night before.

Spirit possession is the most important element in Ainu shamanism. Shamans' spirits are called *tusu kamuy* (shamanistic deity). Despite the designation, however, they are not considered bona fide deities. The exact identity of the spirit helpers, or *kosimpuh*, however, is extremely hard to decipher. Husko, who is otherwise a very eager teacher of the Ainu way, was vague and often peculiarly possessive about the knowledge of spirit helpers. She had to be in the right mood and right physical condition to discuss the subject, since the subject matter was so involved that it might affect her health. Even then she claimed that one cannot express deep knowledge such as that involved in shamanism simply in words, insisting that the only way I could learn about it was to become a shaman myself. Her reluctance to discuss the subject was not due to loss of consciousness during the rites. She claimed that she did not totally lose her consciousness during the rites and expressed suspicion about the claims of other shamans who allegedly could not recall their actions during the rites. Some nondeified animals, such as grasshoppers, crows, ravens, cranes, and ducks, seem to become spirit helpers, although there are also numerous nonanimal spirit helpers such as the aforementioned spirit that likes the aconite roots. Major deities in the Ainu pantheon do not seem to become spirit helpers, although they seem to be the ultimate source of information which the spirit helpers seek to acquire on behalf of the shaman.

The Ainu emphasize that the shamans are entirely passive in that it is the spirit helper which decides more or less haphazardly to possess a particular shaman. No permanent relationship is established between a shaman and a particular spirit. The usual situation seems to be that a shaman has, as it were, a pool of spirits, and one of them possesses him during a particular performance, or it may possess him repeatedly for a certain period of time. Success of a shaman's performance does not rest on one spirit alone. The shaman calls for help to various deities, his guardian deities as well as spirit helpers and guardian deities of his relatives and ancestors. Most important, Grandmother Hearth must mediate. Therefore, a shaman's success depends upon his good relationship with various benevolent beings of the universe.

There are both male and female shamans. Until recently, they were about equal in number, but presently female shamans far outnumber male practitioners. Although the position of shaman as such is not hereditary, the disposition to be a shaman is considered to run in the family. However, not just anyone can become a shaman, nor can one become a shaman simply by desiring to be one. Usually a person starts by experiencing a strong feeling over which he has no control. Most shamans have this experience during their early teens, around the time of puberty, or even earlier. Some years later, often at the time of some life crisis, they may perform their first shamanistic rite, often unconsciously. In the beginning of their career, most shamans perform only when they are seized, but they gradually gain control over themselves and become able to perform only when they wish, often at the request of a client. A shaman's power is believed to gradually increase as his career progresses.

Husko, for example, at about fifteen years of age, started to feel every day at midafternoon a strong desire to sing out loud about anything which came into her mind. At the same time it seemed to her that a strong wind was eddying around inside her body. Her elders told her that she was feeling the desire to perform shamanistic rites. Her first actual performance of a rite did not come, however, until she was 38 years old, when her daughter drowned in a lake at Rayčiska. At the sight of her daughter's dead body caught in a fishnet, she lost consciousness and was carried back to her home. Here she regained consciousness but her body started to shake vigorously. Those present gave her the necessary equipment with which she performed her first rite. Not until her son died several years later, however, did she perform the rites regularly. Another shamaness with whom I became well acquainted in my first field community of Wakasakunai also stated that she started her career when her daughter died.

The Ainu do not regard a shamanistic predisposition as a psychological abnormality or a sign of mental illness. Nor do they perceive the shamans as cunning or mysterious. The Ainu consider the shamans simply as ordinary human beings with a special ability to deal with the deities, and hence pay due respect to them. However, there is no necessary relation between a person's social or economic position and his status as a shaman. Also, notwithstanding a certain amount of economic gain, shamanistic practice alone does not bring fortune to the practitioner. The goods which a client brings are considered to be offerings to the deities and not to the shaman. Therefore, the amount and kinds of offerings are determined by the socioeconomic position of the client rather than by the ability of the shaman. The only occasion when a shaman may receive a sizable amount of wealth is when one of a few wealthy members of his community chooses to consult him about his illness or some comparable problem. On such occasions if the client is male he may offer sheets of leather, shoes, mats, or wooden bowls or even lacquerware obtained from the Japanese; if female, such items as necklaces and shoes of harbor seal skin may be offered. These occasions are rare indeed and usually offerings consist of simple items such as food.

According to the Ainu, the shamans who always engage in sorcery work are found only among other Ainu and other peoples. On the other hand a few shamans on the northwest coast occasionally become possessed by an evil spirit who, without the prior knowledge of the shaman himself, possesses an otherwise benevolent shaman and causes him to engage in malevolent doings. The victim of the sorcery as well as the shaman are at the mercy of the evil spirit, which makes the shaman realize what he has done only after the harm has been accomplished. If male, the victim will vomit blood together with an arrow point and ritual wood shavings. If female, she too will vomit blood, but it will contain a needle and wooden shavings. The relatives of the victim may take revenge by offering the shavings and the arrow tip or the needle to the spirit helper of their own shaman, which in turn is considered to return these objects to the evil shaman so that the latter will consequently be killed by these objects. There is never any kinship relationship between a victim and an evil shaman.

Evil spirits are thought to disguise themselves as birds in traveling to the location of their possible victims. Sagacious elders are consequently always watchful and shoot these birds, which resemble a kite (*Milvus migrans lineatus* [Gray]). They have long claws and large eyes like those of a wildcat and are reddish brown in color with a tinge of gold.

Since the pool of spirits of some shamans include both good and evil spirits, it sometimes happens that a battle between the good and evil spirits takes place within a shaman during his performance. If an evil spirit wins, the shaman falls down on the floor. It is thus the responsibility of people in the audience to help good spirits to win such a battle. The males in the audience thus must swing their daggers to the right and left while shouting, and the women wave branches of fir or ritual sticks made of willow to purify the shaman.

Shamanism as described above presents intriguing contrasts to Ainu nonshamanistic beliefs and rituals. The shamanistic rite is the only individual rite, while all the other rituals of the Ainu are group rituals, requiring the participation of a social unit, either family members or the members of the community, as in the case of the bear ceremony. While the group rituals may never be performed at night, shamanistic rites must be held at night with embers in the hearth as the only source of light. While all other rituals are held outside, shamanistic rites must be held inside the house beside the hearth. In the group rituals, females are barred from active participation and may never be officiators, while both males and females may be shamans. Furthermore, while prayers dedicated during the group ritual are formulaic, those during shamanistic rites are always impromptu, composed by the shamans to suit the occasion. Lastly, crucial in shamanistic performances are spirit helpers, which are not bona fide deities, while the focus of the group rituals is major deities. Although interpretations of these contrasts are beyond the scope of this book, Ainu shamanism presents intriguing questions, since shamanistic belief and practice have remained meaningful to the Ainu to this day, while World War II shattered practically all other religious practices together with most of the Ainu way (for a detailed description of shamanism, see Ohnuki-Tierney 1973a; for interpretations of shamanism, see Ohnuki-Tierney 1973d).

Epilogue

The Ainu way of life as described in this book has almost disappeared; some might say that it has already gone. Although I think that the basic behavioral patterns and cognitive maps of older people, both among the Sakhalin and Hokkaido Ainu, are still those of their own culture, the elders constitute only a small percentage of the Ainu population. Even among the elders, a person like Husko who fully believes in the Ainu way is, indeed, an exception. There is little difference between younger generations of Ainu and Japanese in terms of overt behavior. Both old and young Ainu alike carry out dancing and religious ceremonies often for tourists and for those laymen and scholars who wish to reconstruct the Ainu way.

Many Ainu are now reasserting their cultural identity. In this sense they constitute a social group distinct from that of the Japanese. In this effort some have resorted to drastic measures. For example, a simultaneous bombing in 1972 of an exhibition case containing Ainu artifacts at Hokkaido University in Sapporo and of a group of statues at Asahikawa were done either by "radical" Ainu or by their Japanese sympathizers. The statues had been criticized by Ainu who consider the sitting position of the Ainu figure in contrast to the standing position of the Japanese figures to be an insult to the Ainu. Many Ainu oppose the excavation of Ainu grave sites by archaeologists. Some advocate a revolution and the establishment of an Ainu republic.

The future of Ainu culture is uncertain, and Ainu opinions are divided as to what their future should be. Indeed, there are many parallels between the history of the Ainu and that of the American Indians from the first contact with the "civilized" peoples who claimed their land.

Glossary

Address, term of: A kinship term used when speaking to or addressing a relative.

Affinal: Related by marriage.

Agnates: Male or female descendants by male links.

Amulet: An object that gives supernatural protection to the possessor.

Bilateral: Affiliation traced through both parents and relatives of both sexes.

Consanguineal: Related by "blood" or common ancestry.

Corporate group: A group which controls a body of property and has rules concerning recruitment of members, and whose members have definite rights with respect to each other and to the property.

Descent: The descent rules of a society select certain genealogical attributes and ignore others and affiliate an individual at birth with a group of relatives; this group provides certain rights and obligations.

Ego: In kinship analysis, the person who is used as the reference point for identification of kinship relations and terms.

Exogamy: A rule of practice whereby marriage takes place outside a given group.

Extended family: Composed of two or more nuclear families linked by consanguineal ties.

Family of orientation: One in which an individual is born and reared; it includes his father, mother, and siblings.

Matrilineal: Tracing relationships through females.

Nuclear family: A man, his wife, and his children.

Parallel cousins: The children of a father's brother or a mother's sister.

Patrilineal: Tracing relationships through males.

Patrilocal residence rule: The couple is expected to live either in the home of or in the settlement of the groom's parents.

Reference, term of: A term used in speaking about a relative.

Sibling: One's brother or sister.

Talisman: An object that produces supernatural effects of advantageous character for the possessor.

Teknonymy: A practice whereby a child does not take its name from its parents but rather parents derive a name from their child. For example, an adult is known as "father of so-and-so."

Unilineal: Traced through either a male or a female line of descent.

References

Since the primary sources in Japanese are not readily available to readers, I have included only a few of them. The following list indicates where additional bibliographies may be found.

REFERENCES FOR CHAPTER 1

Birdsell, Joseph B., 1951, "The Problem of the Early Peopling of the Americas as Viewed from Asia." In *The Physical Anthropology of the American Indian*, W. S. Laughlin, ed., pp. 1–68. New York: The Viking Fund, Inc.

Chard, Chester S., 1968, "A New Look at the Ainu Problem," *Proceedings of the Eighth International Congress of Anthropological and Ethnological Sciences*, Vol. III, pp. 98–99. Tokyo: Science Council of Japan.

Fujimoto, Hideo, 1971, *Kita no Haka* (Northern Tombs). Tokyo: Gakuseisha.

Hallowell, A. Irving, 1926, *Bear Ceremonialism in the Northern Hemisphere*. Philadelphia: University of Pennsylvania Press.

Hanihara, Kazuro, 1974, "Dentition of the Ainu and the Australian Aborigines." Paper presented at the Ninth International Congress of Anthropological and Ethnological Sciences, Chicago, 1973. Published by Mouton (The Hague), 1974.

Harrison, John A., 1954, "The Saghalien Trade: A Contribution to Ainu Studies," *Southwestern Journal of Anthropology*, Vol. 10, no. 3, 278–293.

Howells, William W., 1966, "Craniometry and Multivariate Analysis: The Jomon Population of Japan," *Papers of the Peabody Museum of Archaeology and Ethnology*, Vol. LVII, no. 1, 1–43.

Levin, M. G., 1963, *Ethnic Origins of the Peoples of Northeastern Asia* (Arctic Institute of North America, Anthropology of the North. Translations from Russian Sources, no. 3). Toronto: University of Toronto Press.

Omoto, Keiichi, 1974, "Blood Protein in Polymorphisms and the Problem of the Genetic Affinities of the Ainu." Paper presented at the Ninth International Congress of Anthropological and Ethnological Sciences, Chicago, 1973. Published by Mouton (The Hague), 1974.

Sakurai, Kiyohiko, 1967, *Ainu Hishi* (A Hidden History of the Ainu). Tokyo: Kadokawa Shoten.

Spuhler, J. N., 1966, "Numerical Taxonomy and the Ainu Problem." Paper presented at the United States-Japan Cooperative Science Program Seminar, Sapporo, Japan.

Stephan, John J., 1971, *Sakhalin: A History*. Oxford: Clarendon Press.

Street, John C., 1962, Review of *Vergleichende Grammatik der altaischen Sprachen*, by Nikolaus Poppe (1960), *Language*, Vol. 38, no. 1, 92–98.

Takakura, Shinichiro, 1939, "Kinsei ni okeru Karafuto o Chushin to shita Nichiman Koeki" (The Trade between Japan and Manchuria with Reference to Sakhalin in Recent Times [mainly Tokugawa period]), *Hoppo Bunka Kenkyu*, no. 1, 163–194. See Harrison 1954.

Yamaguchi, Bin, 1963a, "Soya-misaki Onkoromanai Kaizuka Shutsudo Jinkotsu" (Human Skeletal Material at the Onkoromanai Shell Mound in Northern Hokkaido), *Jinruigaku Zasshi*, Vol. 70, nos. 3–4, 131–146.

———, 1963b, "Embetsu-gun Tsuishikari Bozuyama Iseki Jinkotsu" (Human Skeletal Material at the Bozuyama Site, Tsuishikari, Embetsu), *Jinruigaku Zasshi*, Vol. 71, no. 2, 55–71.

Yoshizaki, Masakazu, 1963, "Prehistoric Culture in Southern Sakhalin in the Light of Japanese Research," *Arctic Anthropology*, Vol. 1, no. 2, 131–153.

Recommended reading

ETHNOGRAPHIC PUBLICATIONS ON THE AINU

Sakhalin Ainu

There is no ethnographic publication on the northwest coast Ainu other than publications by this author. The following studies are either about the east coast Ainu or the Sakhalin Ainu in general.

Chiri, Mashio, 1944, "Karafuto Ainu no Setsuwa" (Folktales of the Sakhalin Ainu), *Karafutocho Hakubutsukan Iho*, Vol. 3, no. 1, 1–146.
  Along with the folktales, annotations are extremely valuable as ethnographic information.
———, 1953, 1954, 1962, *Bunrui Ainugo Jiten* (Classified Dictionaries of the Ainu Language), 3 vols. (Vol. I—Plants [1953]; Vol. II—Animals [1962]; Vol. III—Humans [1954]). Tokyo: Nihon Jomin Bunka Kenkyujo.
  Each entry includes a description of Ainu terms in different regions in Hokkaido and Sakhalin as well as related ethnographic information. For an exhaustive bibliography of Chiri, see Ohnuki-Tierney (1973b).
———, 1973, "Karafuto Ainu no Seikatsu" (Life of the Sakhalin Ainu), *Chiri Mashio Chosakushu*, Vol. 3, 145–209.
  A short but good account of the life of the Sakhalin Ainu on the east coast.
Fujita, Kiyonobu, 1930, *Karafuto Ainu Kumamatsuri no Kaisetsu* (Sakhalin Ainu Bear Ceremony). Toyohara: Keimosha.
  A brief, but good, account of Sakhalin Ainu bear ceremonialism with valuable photographs.
Harrison, John A., 1955, "Kita Yezo Zusetsu or A Description of the Island of Northern Yezo by Mamiya Rinzo," *Proceedings of the American Philosophical Society*, Vol. 99, no. 2.
  See Mamiya 1855.
Hattori, Shiro, 1957, "Ainugo ni okeru Nenchoshaso Tokushugo" (A Special Language of the Older Generation of the Ainu), *Minzokugaku Kenkyu*, Vol. 21, no. 3, 38–45.
  The author, a linguist, has been intensively studying Husko's speech.
Kindaichi, Kyosuke, 1914, *Kita Ezo Koyo Ihen* (An Ainu Epic of Northern Ezo). Tokyo: Kenkyusha.
  A valuable recording of an epic poem including annotations.
Kondo, Seisai, 1804, *Henyo Bunkai Zuko* (Description of the Frontiers).
  A detailed, accurate description of the northern frontiers of Japan.

Mamiya, Rinzo, 1855, "Kita Ezo Zusetsu" (An Illustrated Description of Northern Ezo). In K. Omoto, ed., *Hokumon Sosho*, Vol. 5, pp. 277–380. Tokyo: Hokko Shobo.
  A good ethnographic description of the Sakhalin Ainu by this famous early explorer. See Harrison (1955) for English translation.

Ohnuki-Tierney, Emiko, 1968, "A Northwest Coast Sakhalin Ainu World View," Ph.D. dissertation, Department of Anthropology, University of Wisconsin, Madison.

———, 1969a, "Concepts of Time among the Ainu of the Northwest Coast of Sakhalin," *American Anthropologist*, Vol. 71, pp. 488–492.

———, 1969b, *Sakhalin Ainu Folklore*, Anthropological Studies No. 2. Washington, D.C.: American Anthropological Association.

———,1972, "Spatial Concepts of the Ainu of the Northwest Coast of Southern Sakhalin, *American Anthropologist*, Vol. 74, pp. 426–455.

———, 1973a, "The Shamanism of the Ainu of the Northwest Coast of Southern Sakhalin, *Ethnology*, Vol. 12, no. 1, 15–29.

———, 1973b (with Hideo Fujimoto), "Mashio Chiri—Ainu Scholar of Ainu Culture and Professor of Linguistics, *American Anthropologist*, Vol. 75, pp. 868–876.

———, 1973c, "Sakhalin Ainu Time Reckoning," *Man*, Vol. 8, no. 2, pp. 285–299.

———, 1973d, "Shamanism and World View—Case of the Ainu of the Northwest Coast of Southern Sakhalin." Paper presented at the Ninth International Congress of Anthropological and Ethnological Sciences, Chicago, 1973. Published by Mouton (The Hague), 1974.

Paproth, Hans-Joachim von, 1970, "Über einige Bärenkultobjekte des Museums für Völkerkunde zu Leipzig," *Jahrbuch des Museums für Völkerkunde zu Leipzig*, Band XXVII, pp. 320–351.
  Valuable photographs taken by Pilsudski of the Sakhalin Ainu are reproduced.

Pilsudski, Bronislov, 1909, "Der Schamanismus bei den Ainu-Stämmen von Sachalin," *Globus*, Vol. 15, no. 4, 261–274; Vol. 16, no. 2, 117–132. (Japanese translation in *Hoppo Bunka Kenkyu Hokoku*, Vol. 16 [1961], pp. 179–203.)
  The best available description of east coast Ainu shamanism.

———, 1912, *Materials for the Study of the Ainu Language and Folklore*. Cracow: Spolka Wydawnicza Polska.
  Valuable annotations are included.

———, 1915, Na medvedž'em prazdnik ajnov o. Sachalina. Žhivaia Starina, Vol. 23 (1914), nos. 1–2, pp. 67–162.
  A very good ethnographic description of Sakhalin Ainu bear ceremonialism.

Sentoku, Taroji, 1929, *Karafuto Ainu Sowa* (The Sakhalin Ainu). Tokyo: Shikodo.
  A brief account of Ainu life by a former chief of the Ainu settlement at Sakaehama on the east coast.

Yamamoto, Toshi, 1968, *Hoppo Shizen Minzoku Minwa Shusei* (A Collection of Folktales of the Northern Peoples). Tokyo: Sagami Shobo.

———, 1971, *Karafuto Ainu Jukyo to Mingu* (Houses and Artifacts of the Sakhalin Ainu). Tokyo: Sagami Shobo.
  A superb ethnographic work about the east coast Ainu.

For further references by these authors and other works on the Sakhalin Ainu, see the bibliographies in publications by Ohnuki-Tierney.

Hokkaido Ainu and Ainu in General

Ainu Bunka Hozon Taisaku Kyogikai (Committee on the Protection of Ainu Culture), ed., 1970, *Ainu Minzokushi* (The Ainu). Tokyo: Daiichihoki Shuppan.

A comprehensive survey of Ainu culture, language, and the problem of Ainu identity. The Ainu in each region are discussed under each topic, although there is only limited coverage of the Sakhalin Ainu under such topics as religion and social structure. The numerous photographs are valuable even to readers who do not read Japanese.

Batchelor, John, 1927, *Ainu Life and Lore*. Tokyo: Kyobunkan.
The author's missionary background and the nineteenth century evolutionary concept influence his writings in areas such as religion.

Hallowell, A Irving, 1926, *Bear Ceremonialism in the Northern Hemisphere*. Philadelphia: University of Pennsylvania.
Ainu bear ceremonialism is discussed in reference to similar practices of peoples in the circumpolar regions.

Ifube, Masao, 1969, *Saru Ainu no Kumamatsuri* (The Bear Ceremony of the Saru Ainu).
A comprehensive account of the bear ceremony of the Saru Ainu of Hokkaido.

Kanenari, Matsu, 1959–1965, *Ainu Jojishi Yukarashu* (A Collection of Ainu Epic Poems), 5 vols. Tokyo: Sanseido.
The author, an Ainu woman, wrote these valuable Ainu texts of epic poems in phonemic notation. Japanese translation is included.

Kindaichi, Kyosuke, 1925, *Ainu no Kenkyu* (Study of the Ainu). Tokyo: Naigai Shobo.

———, 1944, *Ainu Yukara Itadorimaru no Kyoku* (Ainu Epic Poem, *Kutune Shirka*). Tokyo: Seijisha.
This lengthy epic poem is presented in Ainu phonemic notation. Japanese translation and valuable annotations are included.

Kitagawa, Joseph M., 1961, "Ainu Bear Festival (*Iyomante*)." In *History of Religion*, Vol. 1, no. 1, 95–151.
General discussion of Ainu prehistory and culture along with the bear ceremonialism of the Saru Ainu at Piratori, Hokkaido.

Munro, Neil Gordon, 1963, *Ainu Creed and Cult*. New York: Columbia University Press.
An excellent work on the religion of the Saru Ainu at Nibutani, Hokkaido. Seligman's discussion of the social structure and bear ceremony, which she compiled from Munro's notes, are valuable additions.

Nihon Minzokugaku Kyokai, ed., 1952, "Saru Ainu Kyodo Chosa Hokoku" (Report of the Joint Research on the Saru Ainu), *Minzokugaku Kenkyu*, Vol. 16, nos. 3–4.
Results of intensive investigations conducted by various specialists.

Sugiura, Kenichi, and Harumi Befu, 1962, "Kinship Organization of the Saru Ainu," *Ethnology*, Vol. 1, no. 3, 287–298.

Takakura, Shinichiro, 1960, "The Ainu of Northern Japan: A Study in Conquest and Acculturation," *Transactions of the American Philosophical Society*, N.S., Vol. 50, Part 4.

———, 1966, "Vanishing Ainu of Northern Japan," *Natural History* (Oct.), pp. 16–25.

Watanabe, Hitoshi, 1964, "The Ainu—A Study of Ecology and the System of Social Solidarity between Man and Nature in Relation to Group Structure," *Journal of the Faculty of Science*, University of Tokyo, Vol. II, Sec. V, Part 6. Republished as *The Ainu Ecosystem*, 1973. Seattle, Wash.: University of Washington Press.

Kurile Ainu

Torii, Ryuzo, 1919, "Études Archéologiques et Ethnologiques des Ainou des Îles Kouriles," *Journal of the College of Science*, Tokyo Imperial University, Vol. XLII, Article 1.

For earlier publications in Western languages, see the bibliographies in Hallowell (1926) and Kitagawa (1961).

Films and music

AINU FILMS AVAILABLE IN THE UNITED STATES

"Iyomande—The Ainu Bear Festival." Black and white. Sound (English). 26 minutes. 16 mm.
    An excellent movie about the bear festival of the Ainu in the Saru River Valley in Hokkaido, filmed by Munro in the early 1930s. For a written account of the festival, see Munro (1963:169–171). Distributed by the University of California Extension Media Center, Berkeley, California 94702.
"Canoes of the Ainu." Color. Sound (English). 19 minutes.
    Includes the making of a canoe and the accompanying ritual, dancing, and singing of the Hokkaido Ainu. Distributed by American Educational Films, 9879 Santa Monica Blvd., Beverly Hills, California 90212.
"The Gods of the Ainu." Color. Sound (English). 16 minutes.
    Focuses on the Hokkaido Ainu gods as honorary guests and revered protectors of the Ainu.

AINU MUSIC

Ainu Dento Ongaku (Ainu Traditional Music). 2 vols. 1965. Sapporo: Nihon Hoso Kyokai.
    This is an excellent collection of traditional music of both the Hokkaido and Sakhalin Ainu.